PRAYING WITH
WOMEN
OF THE
BIBLE

Also by Nancy Kennedy

PRAYING WITH
WOMEN
OF THE
BIBLE

NANCY KENNEDY

ZONDERVAN™

GRAND RAPIDS, MICHIGAN 49530 USA

ZONDERVAN™

Praying with Women of the Bible
Copyright © 2004 by Nancy Kennedy

Requests for information should be addressed to:

Zondervan, *Grand Rapids, Michigan 49530*

Library of Congress Cataloging-in-Publication Data

Kennedy, Nancy, 1954–.
    Praying with women of the Bible / Nancy Kennedy.—1ˢᵗ ed.
       p. cm.
    Includes index.
    ISBN 0-310-25222-9
    1. Women in the Bible. 2. Women—Prayer-books and devotions—
English. I. Title.
BS575.K46 2003
248.3'2—dc22

                                2003018765
                                     CIP

Published in association with the literary agency of Ann Spangler and Company, 1420 Pontiac Road S.E., Grand Rapids, MI 49506.

Interior design by Michelle Espinoza

Printed in the United States of America

---

04 05 06 07 08 09 10 /❖ DC/ 10 9 8 7 6 5 4 3 2 1

*This book is dedicated to Caroline Kennedy Smith,
my favorite first granddaughter. May God surprise
and delight you as he answers your prayers.*

TABLE OF CONTENTS

ACKNOWLEDGMENTS

It sounds so clichéd to say that I couldn't have written this book without others' help, but that's the truth.

My first acknowledgment goes to Ann Spangler, my agent, who feeds me great ideas and then as I run wild with them, reins me in until I find my focus. She's amazing. From cover design and title to back of the book copy, her ideas and guidance shine through. Thank you, Ann.

Next, I want to thank Sandy Vander Zicht, an extraordinary editor at Zondervan. Sandy understands my unconventional, cockeyed way of approaching life and has encouraged me to be myself in my writing. I also want to thank my other Zondervan editor, Verlyn Verbrugge, whom I've never met but hope to some day. The whole Zondervan team so far has been amazing to work with.

I definitely couldn't do what I do without the love and care from my church family at Seven Rivers Presbyterian Church in Lecanto, Florida. I am beyond grateful to them (and the preacher's not half-bad, either).

Thanks, too, to my dear friends and cheerleaders Steve Brown and Charlie Wade. Somehow my name found its way onto their daily prayer lists, and Lord knows I need all the prayer I can get! Steve's wisdom is as deep as his voice, and so is my gratitude to him for listening to my "saga thus far."

There isn't enough space to express my gratitude to my husband, Barry Kennedy, who gives me all the freedom I have ever needed to write books. His fee is quite fair, too. He's another amazing person in my life.

That said, my deepest thanks go to the most amazing One of all: Gracious Holy God, you who know me at my worst, yet still continue to use and bless me. I will never cease to be amazed by your grace!

SURPRISED BY PRAYER

I have a confession to make. By nature, I'm a skeptic. When it comes to prayer, I pray because I should — because the Bible tells me to — but it doesn't come easily. I know God answers prayer because I've seen him do it countless times, but I don't know why he does it or how he does it.

I remember when my daughter Alison was about three. As a new Christian learning to pray, I attempted to teach her to pray too. Actually, at that time I was trying to teach her about "giving money to Jesus." She had put fifty cents of her own in the offering plate at church on a Sunday morning, then misplaced one of her shoes that afternoon. We hadn't discovered that bit of information until the next morning during our frantic rush to get out the door for preschool.

Only after turning the house upside down trying to find the missing shoe did I think to pray. Alison and I knelt down, put our faces on the couch, and in earnest asked, "Dear God, you know where Alison's shoe is and we don't. Please show us so we can get to school on time. Amen."

As a skeptic, I didn't expect God to answer our prayer. Although I knew that he knew the whereabouts of the shoe, I considered it a trivial matter to the Creator of the heavens. I had prayed because I thought I should set an example for my child.

After our "Amen," Alison immediately ran to my bedroom and found her shoe under my bed — with a dollar bill in it. "Jesus found my shoe, and Jesus gave me money just like I gave him!" she squealed. It was a complete and utter surprise to me.

Sometimes the simplest occurrences prove to be the most profound. That answer to my simple request gave me my first real glimpse into the God to whom we pray and into prayer itself. It stirred my skepticism and started me on a quest filled with questions:

- What is prayer and does it really make a difference? How should I pray? What should I pray for? Is there a right way (or a wrong way) to pray?
- Will God really hear my prayers — and will he answer? Or are his "answers" merely coincidences?
- How much faith does prayer require? How long should I pray about something before giving up? Should I ever give up?
- The list goes on.

I imagine you have a list of your own questions, too. That's because prayer is one of those nebulous things, like faith, that defy logic. On the one hand, throughout the Bible God has demonstrated that he works both independently of any human being as well as through the prayers of his people. "I am the LORD," he says repeatedly. He is without rival, holy, almighty. He is to be feared.

On the other hand, he is a God who condescends to listen to the prayers of his children and often doesn't act without them. So he bids us to approach his throne with the boldness of a much-loved child to make our requests known.

But prayer is so much more than telling God what we want. From the examples of God's people recorded in the

Bible, prayer ranges from wordless groans of anguish and cries of lament to songs of worship and praise.

- Moses prayed on behalf of a rebellious people.
- Elijah prayed for rain.
- Jabez prayed to receive a blessing and to be a blessing.
- David prayed for forgiveness and praised the Lord because he had received it.
- Jesus prayed, "Not as I will, but as you will."

In addition to the prayers of these great men, Scripture also records the prayers of women who sought the Lord. Deborah, a prophetess and judge in Israel and a mother who was willing to serve God, sang a song of victory after she helped defeat the Canaanite army. Anna, another prophetess, prayed in the temple diligently and continually for more than sixty years. One woman, whose name we never learn but whose desperation we can understand, reached out in faith to Jesus, saying, "If I just touch the hem of his garment."

Although the prayers of these ancient women don't hold any secrets that need to be unlocked or contain formulas that, if followed, guarantee God will answer in a certain way, they do provide assurances that a child of God can come to him with any and every need and be accepted.

In prayer, we wrestle with our willingness to obey and ask for daily bread. We confess our sins and share our dreams, plead for mercy and laugh with delight. In prayer, we can even bring God our misguided requests and selfish ambitions. That's not saying we get whatever we ask for, only that we have complete freedom to ask without the fear of condemnation.

If there's a secret to prayer, this may be it: We are free to ask. Sometimes, however, we need encouragement — to keep on asking, to keep on praying. It's not that we don't know how to pray, it's that we tire easily, get discouraged, and give up. We don't need a lecture on why we should pray; we need someone to come alongside of us to tell us to keep going. Often the best encouragement in prayer is found in the company of others who pray. *If they can do it, I can do it.*

This book examines the prayers of ten women found in the Bible, beginning with Deborah. Like you and I, these women weren't perfect. Perfect people have no need of prayer, only people who have doubts and fears, who worry about paying the bills, and who cry over their kids. Prayer is for those with great faith as well as for skeptics who shake their heads in amazement when God tucks a dollar bill inside a little girl's shoe and hides it under her mother's bed so that both will be driven to their knees.

Prayer is for those who know their greatest resource is found at the throne of the King, reserved for those who have been given the right to call him Father.

Prayer is for people like you and me.

May this book encourage us both as we approach God's throne together.

The Prayer of Deborah
She Prayed with Strength and Conviction

*So may all your enemies perish, O LORD! But may they
who love you be like the sun when it rises in its strength.*
Judges 5:31

*L ord, I will go anywhere you lead (except Africa, or Cincinnati).
I will do anything you ask (but please don't ask me to work in
the nursery). I am your willing servant (although "servant" sounds
awfully lowly; how about "kingdom colleague"?). May your will be
done in my life (as long as it's not too inconvenient). Amen.*

While I've never actually prayed a prayer like that, if
God read my heart (which he can and does), he would know
that often when I say I'm willing, I'm really not. To give
myself wholeheartedly to a God I cannot see and who may
ask me to do something disruptive and discomforting is
scary. I may have to leave the security of my everyday rou-
tine or the comfort of my self-sufficient life. I may have to
walk by faith when I'd much rather walk by sight.

If I give myself to God, he may lead me to greatness,
which is a terrifying thought. Mediocrity is so much more

comfortable than adventure and risk. Give me white bread and vanilla pudding any day. Foggy, drizzly days, sitting on my couch. Sipping lukewarm decaf instant coffee, munching on bland saltine crackers, working on crossword puzzles. A life without challenges. Ahhhhh!

The trouble with that is, once God has called us into his kingdom through faith in Christ, he gives us his Spirit, who stirs us out of our comfortable complacency. "I've come that you might have life," he whispers. "I've got a grand plan, adventures and opportunities you never dreamed possible."

He addresses our fear and reluctance. "Don't be afraid," he says. And then, just as Jesus did with Peter, his disciple, he tells us to do something outrageous, such as "Get out of the boat you're in and walk on water." That's when either we run for the comfort of our couch, grab the TV remote, and flip on *Jeopardy!* or we arise and follow God's call.

A MOTHER IN ISRAEL AROSE

Only nine in the morning, and I've already listened to three disputes over stolen donkeys, Deborah thought as she reviewed her list of cases for the day. As a prophetess of God, and the only woman to serve as a judge in Israel, sometimes she felt torn between her duties at home as a wife and mother and her duties as one of God's chosen leaders for his people. Sometimes, she wondered if these stubborn Israelites were even worth leading.

After Joshua died, the generations that followed did evil in the sight of the Lord by serving foreign gods, including Deborah's generation. God chastised them by allowing them to be ruled by their enemies. At the time Deborah served as judge, with her "courtroom" under a palm tree in the hill country of Ephraim, the Israelites had already lived twenty years under the cruel oppression of Jabin, a Canaanite king, and Sisera, the commander of Jabin's army.

To Deborah, it seemed the more oppressed the Israelites felt, the more they took it out on each other. She had noticed her caseload growing daily: neighbor versus neighbor, relatives disputing relatives. *And over such trivial things*, she thought. *Even my youngest children know how to share their toys!*

The men had also turned cowardly or complacent. She didn't know which it was, or maybe it was both. There had been chatter lately about Sisera's nine hundred iron chariots and about how the Israelites had none. The men, and the women too, spent long hours complaining to each other — complaining about each other — but not one of them offered to do anything about anything.

After the last case of the day was settled, Deborah stood up and stretched. She had sensed a restlessness in her spirit all day, and she knew it wasn't from listening to squabbles about property lines or whose donkey belonged to whom. She had learned long ago how to keep her work from robbing her of the peace God had given her. No, this restlessness she felt seemed to come from God himself, as if he was disturbing her peace.

The people had been crying out for a leader — someone to be their champion, their deliverer, their savior, from their enemy. Someone like Joshua, they had been saying. However, for all of the men's many words and heartfelt laments, even when they turned their cries to the Lord for help, not one Israelite man stepped forward to lead the people.

That's when Deborah sensed God calling her to be the one to rise up. In a culture dominated by men, Deborah knew the risk she would be taking to volunteer as leader. It was difficult enough serving as judge! Some of the men who appeared before her bench didn't appreciate being told what to do by a "mere woman," as she had been called.

How can I be a leader against Sisera? she thought. *I'm not a warrior; I'm just a mom!*

Still, her spirit remained restless until she finally relented. "Okay, God," she said. "I don't know exactly what you want me to do — or even why you would want to use me — but there's no one else who's willing."

As soon as she spoke those words, God's peace returned, and she breathed deeply. "Thank you, Lord," she whispered.

Next, the Lord began to speak to Deborah and to give her his instructions. After Deborah had heard from God, she sent for Barak, a fellow Israelite, and instructed him to gather ten thousand men from the tribes of Naphtali and Zebulun and go to Mount Tabor. Then she would lure Sisera to the Kishon River and into Barak's hands.

However, Barak was afraid. "If you go with me, I will go," he told her. "But if you don't go with me, I won't go" (Judges 4:8).

Deborah agreed, but told him that because of his request, the honor of victory wouldn't be his, "for the LORD will hand Sisera over to a woman."

Barak and Deborah gathered the ten thousand men, and "at Barak's advance, the LORD routed Sisera and all his chariots and army by the sword." Sisera himself fled on foot and escaped into the tent of a woman named Jael. There, once he had fallen asleep, Jael drove a tent peg through his skull (Judges 4:4–21).

After the Israelite's victory, Deborah sang this prayer of praise:

> When the princes in Israel take the lead,
> when the people willingly offer themselves —
> praise the LORD! (Judges 5:2)

In the days of Shamgar son of Anath,
> in the days of Jael, the roads were abandoned;
> travelers took to winding paths.

Village life in Israel ceased,
> ceased until I, Deborah, arose,
> arose a mother in Israel. (Judges 5:6–7)

After that, Israel was at peace for forty years.

The Bible doesn't say anything else about Deborah. We don't know about her home, her husband, or her children. All we know is that when she heard from God, she arose. She was willing to heed the voice of God spurring her toward service. And as she arose, so did the men of Israel. Together, they witnessed God's power routing their enemies in the face of overwhelming odds. Together they enjoyed a decades-long peace. Twice in her song she commends those who rose up with her and offered themselves in service to the Lord. "My heart is with Israel's princes," she sang, "with the willing volunteers among the people. Praise the LORD!" (Judges 5:9).

WHAT, ME WILLING?

Deborah heard from God and believed him. She trusted that whatever he told her was true and that he would keep his word. She knew him, she knew his character. She had heard the stories of his faithfulness to Abraham and Sarah, to Joseph, to Moses, and to Joshua. She had heard the stories of how the Lord parted the Red Sea so the Israelites could escape slavery in Egypt and how he fed them for forty years as they wandered in the desert.

She heard of his patience with his people and how he came to their rescue when they cried out to him. She knew of his compassion and his great love. Even if she were afraid —

and who wouldn't be if they were faced with an enemy with nine hundred chariots? — because she knew God's character, she knew she could trust him with whatever he might call her to do. Those who know God, even if they are afraid, willingly step out on faith to follow him — sometimes with bold leaps, other times with tentative steps.

> *Those who know God, even if they are afraid, willingly step out on faith to follow him — sometimes with bold leaps, other times with tentative steps.*

When Jesus came to Peter, walking on the surface of a lake, Peter and the other disciples in the boat were terrified. The wind was against them and the waves buffeted the boat. When Jesus appeared in the distance approaching them, they thought he was a ghost.

Jesus told them not to be afraid. "It is I," he said.

That's all he needed to say. They had spent time with him and knew his character. Peter, one who knew him best, said, "Lord, if it's really you, then tell me to walk on water too."

Jesus told him, "Come."

The gospel of Matthew records that Peter climbed out of the boat and took several steps toward Jesus. Can you imagine what that was like? Terrifying and exhilarating all at once. *Look at me! I'm walking — on water! Can you believe it?*

But then when he saw the wind, his fear won out over his faith, and he began to sink. He cried out, "Lord, save me!"

Jesus did. He reached out his hand and kept him from drowning. Then he asked Peter, "Why did you doubt?" (Matthew 14:22–31).

When it comes to being willing to step out on faith, to heed God's call on our lives, why do we doubt? Why do *you* doubt?

Why do I?

I remember a job I had years ago. With two young daughters at home and a desire to earn extra money, I took a job doing machine appliqué sewing at home, for which I was paid piecework. Eventually, the job took over my life. If I wasn't at my sewing machine doing the actual sewing, then I was cutting fabric or assembling pieces for the next day's work or trimming completed pieces from the previous day.

I did this for several years and averaged only ten dollars a day, seven days a week. Out of that seventy dollars, I still had to pay taxes, so I probably only made sixty. If I divide that by the number of hours I spent working, I come up with an hourly rate of less than a dollar.

God knew this. He also knew he had something better for me. However, I didn't know that. I was like the disciples in the boat, terrified at the raging storm but unwilling to step out.

Every morning as I sat down at my sewing machine, I heard the voice of Jesus urging, "Come. Quit the job that pays so little and takes up so much of your time and trust that I have something better."

But I wouldn't. I was unwilling ... and afraid. I thought we needed that seventy dollars a week. Money was tight enough with it, and I didn't think we could survive without it.

So I resisted the Lord for another two years. I knew I didn't trust that his love and faithfulness would be sufficient, and that made me feel guilty. I kept thinking, "What if my child didn't trust me? What if my daughter doubted my goodness and my love?"

I resist God and become unwilling to surrender to him because I'm not convinced that he loves me — it's a control issue. I'm unwilling to give up control of my life because I don't think anyone else, including God, can take care of me the way I can.

Some call this *orphan thinking*. Orphans fend for themselves and take control of their surroundings. After all, who else will? They are distrustful and unwilling to give themselves to anyone. But for those of us who have been adopted by the Father through faith in Jesus, there is no need to think or act like an orphan.

I have a Father who loves me lavishly and cares for me deeply. A Father who loves me with an everlasting love, who delights in me, and who rejoices over me. When I forget that, I shrink back in fear. When I am afraid, I hold onto whatever I think will make me feel secure, such as a job that doesn't bring me pleasure or satisfaction; I'm afraid to let go.

WILLING? NO . . .
BUT WILLING TO BE MADE WILLING? YES!

After resisting God for two years, I finally gave in. Wrestling with the Almighty is tiring and pointless; you always lose. Except, when you lose to God, you end up winning.

> *Wrestling with the Almighty is tiring and pointless; you always lose. Except, when you lose to God, you end up winning.*

One Friday I prayed: "Lord, I want to be willing, but I'm not. I'm afraid. But I'm also miserable. If you change my heart, I will do whatever you say." My prayer may have been filled with doubt and fear, but it was honest. I wasn't willing, but I was willing to be made willing.

Scripture says God "works in you to will and to act according to his good purpose" (Philippians 2:13). He makes us willing and then he empowers us to do whatever he intends.

By Monday morning, I couldn't wait to call the woman I worked for to tell her it was my last week of sewing. I felt as if I were walking on water, terrified yet exhilarated. I had no idea what lay ahead. I only knew that Jesus had bid me, "Come." So I took a breath and stepped out of the boat.

As it turned out, that was a pivotal point in my life. Shortly after I quit my sewing job, I began writing stories for Christian magazines, which led to having several books published, which led to a speaking ministry, which led to greater opportunities to trust God to care for me.

ARISE — AND SHINE!

Willingness to follow Jesus doesn't guarantee success as we may define success. According to tradition, all of Christ's original disciples except one ended up dying violently because they chose to follow him. However, not many of us are called to die a martyr's death. But we are called to die to ourselves daily and to give our lives away for the sake of the kingdom.

What happens when I willingly give myself to God? I experience an inner calm because I stop striving. Even in the face of opposition, I can do what's right because I'm at peace with God. Also, my faith and trust in him increases. As he proves himself trustworthy, I trust him more. As I trust him more, I am more willing to give myself to him. I may even walk on water if he asks me to because I know he won't let me drown.

Deborah sang a song of victory. She could have stayed under the palm tree judging disputes among the people, but she arose, "a mother in Israel," and willingly followed God's lead into battle. Because she did, she saw him utterly destroy her enemies and oppressors. She sang,

So may all your enemies perish, O LORD!
But may they who love you be like the sun
when it rises in its strength. (Judges 5:31)

We all battle enemies. Sometimes our enemies are real, human enemies who threaten our safety and well-being. Sometimes the enemy is a philosophy that threatens to suppress or even overthrow the truth we believe as revealed by God in the Bible.

Our enemies are often unseen, yet so very real, threatening our peace and destroying relationships, our communities, our nation, our world. We're afraid to do battle, and afraid not to. Yet, for those who belong to God through faith in his Son, Jesus, our enemies become his enemies. With God on our side, our enemies don't stand a chance of ultimate victory.

That doesn't mean we go unscathed; it just means we win in the end. Just as Deborah prayed, we who love God and are loved by him are "like the sun when it rises in its strength."

We shine.

God often calls his children into battle, though not many of our battles involve something as risky as leading a nation into war. More often, he calls us to battle our complacency and fear and plain old unwillingness to move from a place of comfort. He calls us to step out in faith to lead a backyard Bible club for the neighborhood kids or share our faith with a neighbor. He calls us to love an abrasive coworker or show grace to a prodigal child or a difficult husband. He calls us out of security and sameness and into uncertainty and adventure, prodding us higher, farther, and deeper in relationship with him and with those around us.

Many times, that's where the biggest battles lie.

If you want to experience God working more deeply in your life, take a few moments now and throughout the weeks ahead to pray Deborah's prayer in your own words. As you do, ask God to remind you that he is capable of turning your fear and unwillingness into faith and fervor. Remember, too, that he equips and empowers those whom he calls and then goes with us so that we need never be alone.

Just as he did with Deborah, he does for us: fights our battles, slays our enemies, and then gives us a song to sing. All we have to do is arise.

Lord,

On my own, my strength is puny and my convictions waver — except when it comes to exercising my own will! But your Word says to trust in you with my whole heart, and "lean not" on my own understanding, and in everything I do, acknowledge you.

I know that if you lead me to do something, you will provide the necessary strength — even the strength to do something I really don't want to do. But I also know that when I lack the willingness and the conviction, you can and will change my heart.

It's a scary and awesome thing, the way you take ordinary people like Deborah — like me — and call them to do extraordinary things. Lord, make me willing and then make me able to do whatever you call me to do.

I want to rise like the sun, in your strength, and shine for your glory. Because I know your goodness and your mercy, I offer myself to you as an act of worship.

In Jesus' name. Amen.

DIGGING DEEPER

Think: If God is calling you to do something that you have been unwilling to do, what are your doubts and fears about it?

Study: Romans 12:1–8

Apply: Create your own prayer of surrender and willingness, using Deborah's life and prayer as an example. Read her story in Judges 4–5.

Consider: Deborah sang about the victory that God gave her and her people over their enemies, and so can we.

Reflect: "Expect great things *from* God. Attempt great things *for* God."–William Carey

The Prayer of Hannah
She Prayed for Help

O Lord Almighty . . .
look upon your servant's misery and remember me.
1 Samuel 1:11

As the late Gilda Radner said, "It's always something." We all have something in our lives that God uses to drive us to our knees before him. For some, it's a chronic illness or chronic pain. For others it's financial woes, a difficult marriage, or a relative that irritates like sandpaper. For still others it's a wayward child, a habit that has us in its grip, a shattered dream, or an unmet desire.

For Hannah, it was her barrenness.

More than a woman's role or even a duty, in ancient Hebrew society it was a woman's moral obligation and responsibility to marry and bear her husband sons. Infertility was viewed as a disgrace. A barren woman brought shame and reproach to her husband, his family, her family. The responsibility of continuing her husband's family line fell to her. If she could not produce children, she faced the possibility of divorce. At the least, she faced the rejection of society.

Hannah knew this to the core of her being. As she maneuvered her way through the marketplace, she felt the scorn of the other women and fought back the tears as she tried to ignore the whispers of the gossipers. "What grievous sin did Hannah commit that God would close her womb?" they cackled to each other.

Others clutched their children close to their sides and crossed to the other side of the street when they saw her approach, in case her "curse" should rub off on them. To be infertile was seen as disfavored by God.

To compound Hannah's bitter sorrow over being childless, Peninnah, Hannah's husband's other wife, had children and took great delight in lording it over Hannah. "Be a dear, and get me a drink of water, Han. I'm so tired; you know how it is when you're pregnant. Oops, you don't. My mistake," she taunted.

Not even being the favorite wife of Elkanah eased Hannah's emotional pain. She was helpless, hopeless, desperate, and in despair. God had closed her womb, and only God could help her.

LOOK UPON ME, LORD!

Years earlier, Sarah had also been barren. But Sarah had a plan. Mistakenly believing that "God helps those who help themselves," she set out to conceive a son for her husband, Abraham. Even though they were both well past the child-producing years, God had promised the couple offspring and a legacy, a lineage and a family more numerous than the stars. However, after years of no signs of pregnancy, Sarah offered her maid, Hagar, to Abraham as a surrogate to bear Abraham's child in Sarah's place.

Instead of going to God in her helplessness and waiting for him to fulfill his promise in his time, Sarah stepped in with her own brand of "help." Hagar conceived and gave birth to Ishmael, who became the father of the Arab-Islamic world and enemy to the Jews throughout history — even to this day.

In contrast, Hannah did not take matters into her own hands, as Sarah had done. Instead, Hannah went to the tabernacle to pour out her heart to the Lord. As the author of 1 Samuel describes, Hannah wept "in bitterness of soul" as she prayed and pleaded, vowing, "O LORD Almighty, if you will only look upon your servant's misery and remember me, and not forget your servant but give her a son, then I will give him to [you]" (1 Samuel 1:11).

Hannah knew she could not help herself. She did, however, know the One who could help her, the One who takes great pity on those who turn to him in

Hannah knew she could not help herself. She did, however, know the One who could help her, the One who takes great pity on those who turn to him in their need.

their need. As she wept and cast herself before the Lord in utter dependence on his mercy, she did so trusting that he would hear her cry and look upon her and that he would come to her rescue and be her help.

GOD RIDES A TRACTOR LAWN MOWER

When I first met Cindy, she and her husband had just relocated from Pennsylvania, moving into the house around the bend from mine. With a new baby and an active five-year-old, Cindy was eager to start a new life in Florida. Her husband had struggled with drug and alcohol addiction and had also been unfaithful to her. The move to Florida was his promise to her that he wanted to break old habits and start fresh.

Sadly, his promise to Cindy lasted less than two weeks. He told her he loved her and their children, but he wasn't ready or willing to give up the girlfriend he had left behind. They hadn't even unpacked when Cindy's husband went back to Pennsylvania.

For the next two years, Cindy juggled raising her children alone with working part-time and going to school as well. During that time, my friend rode an emotional roller coaster, believing one day that God could and would restore her marriage and family, and the next day crying hopelessly for hours.

Then came the request for a divorce. Cindy had loved her husband through the years of his drug use, his alcoholism, even his unfaithfulness. She had prayed and trusted, hoped and believed. The day the papers came in the mail, Cindy bottomed out. Her dog had died a few days before, she had a pile of bills she couldn't pay, her son had been experiencing emotional problems, and now she faced the reality that she was being abandoned by the man she still loved.

Feeling completely out of control, Cindy decided to mow her lawn; it was the one thing in her world that she felt she could do. However, her lawn mower refused to start. She fiddled with the knobs awhile, but nothing happened. That's when she snapped. She began screaming and cursing heavenward, then threw herself onto her overgrown lawn and wailed.

"Where are you?" she demanded of God. "You said you would be my Husband; you said you would be my help. I need you! Where are you?"

Almost immediately, Cindy heard the sound of a tractor lawn mower rounding the bend, with an elderly man driving it. Seeing Cindy crying next to her own lawn mower, he stopped to ask if he could help. Wiping her drippy nose with her dirty arm, all she could do was nod.

The man not only got her lawn mower started, but he sent her inside to take a shower while he mowed her grass for her.

Later, she called to tell me what had happened. "God came to help me, riding on a tractor lawn mower!" she said.

Her situation hadn't changed, but because God had come to her aid, meeting her at her point of utter helplessness, she felt hopeful. God had revealed himself to Cindy as her "refuge and strength, an ever-present help in trouble" (Psalm 46:1). She still had bills that needed to be paid, a family pet to be mourned, and children who missed their father, not to mention an uncertain future as a divorcée, but God had looked upon her and remembered her as he had done with Hannah.

O GOD, HEAR MY CRY FOR HELP!

Hannah needed help. Unlike today, she didn't have the benefits of modern medicine to help her conceive, and she desperately wanted a child.

As she did every year, she had traveled with Elkanah and Peninnah from their home in Ramathaim to worship the Lord at the tabernacle in Shiloh. Every year the same thing would happen: Peninnah would make it a point to provoke Hannah to tears. This year, however, Hannah could bear it no longer.

As the family finished eating, perhaps Hannah looked around at Peninnah nursing her youngest child and Elkanah bouncing a toddler on his knee. *I'm an outcast in my own family,* she thought. Feeling utterly alone and forsaken, her heart broke. Her arms ached to hold a child, and she knew just where to go to find relief.

She held back her tears until she was sure she was alone in the presence of the Lord, and then with wails of grief and bitter anguish, she poured out her heart to the only One who could satisfy her longing. As she moved her lips in silent prayer, Eli the priest took notice.

There's nothing worse than a drunken female, he thought. "Woman, you're drunk!" he scoffed. "Get rid of your wine" (1 Samuel 1:12–14, paraphrase mine).

Assuring him she had not been drinking, Hannah told Eli of her need and of her prayer to the Lord for help.

"[Then] go in peace," he told her, "and may the God of Israel grant you what you have asked of him" (1 Samuel 1:17).

Hannah gasped. *Has God heard my prayer?* she wondered. As she wiped her face with her apron, she began to feel hopeful that God truly had heard and that he would either give her a child or would satisfy her desires with himself. With a hint of a smile on her face, she left the tabernacle.

The next morning, Hannah and her husband worshiped before the Lord, then returned home to Ramah. Afterwards "Elkanah lay with Hannah his wife, *and the LORD remembered her*" (1 Samuel 1:19, emphasis mine).

Soon after that, Hannah conceived and gave birth to the great Samuel, who grew to be a man blessed by the Lord and destined to become the last judge in Israel and the one God chose to anoint David as king.

God had closed Hannah's womb for many years, but he hadn't closed his heart to her cries. Neither does he ignore the cries of any of his children who call on him in their helplessness. He comes to our rescue, not always to change our circumstances but always to change our focus from ourselves to him.

In Cindy's case, God came to her rescue, but he didn't change her circumstances right away. Although he continued and still continues to be her help, she struggled greatly for several years as she went through the process of divorce and readjusting her life as a single mother. Today she says she cherishes that time because without it, she would never have known the riches of God's grace to her in her time of need.

HELP FOR THOSE WHO HELP THEMSELVES

Not everyone's life is in crisis all the time. We are not always in tears before the Lord, begging for his help. Sometimes life works. Maybe your life works right now. You've got your health; your bills are paid. Your husband's kisses still make your heart pound; your kids' crises are manageable.

Your faith is secure. You know that you can always call on God if you need his help. But right now, you don't. You're doing fine without it. However, needing God's help isn't solely for the desperate. Sometimes we need his help most when we're least aware of our need.

I used to drive a ten-year-old red Ford Tempo with 189,000 miles on it. For the last two years I drove it, a noise that sounded like metal contracting and expanding drove me crazy. But because my mechanic couldn't find anything wrong, I shrugged it off and continued driving it.

When I bought a new car, I gave the Tempo to a woman I work with. She drove it home, parked it in her yard — and the engine fell out! For those two years I had driven the car completely unaware that three out of the four bolts that hold the engine to the block had fallen off. The noise had been caused by the weight of the engine straining the remaining bolt!

All that time I was unaware of my need for help, but I was nonetheless in need. How grateful I am that God came to my rescue and helped me even when I thought all was well.

It's like that with my spiritual life sometimes, too. I've never consciously said, "Lord, everything is going smoothly so today, I'm going to stop trusting you for my daily needs." For me, for most of us, it's more of a subtle, gradual drifting. It begins with going all day or all week without opening my Bible. *I know what it says*, I tell myself. *I have God's Word in my heart*. Then I notice my prayer life waning. Eventually, unless I'm careful, it becomes nearly nonexistent.

> *I've never consciously said, "Lord, everything is going smoothly, so today I'm going to stop trusting you for my daily needs." For me, for most of us, it's more of a subtle, gradual drifting.*

Even though I know God is in his heaven and all is well, when I'm not aware of my utter dependence on him for each breath I take, I become disconnected from him. When that happens, there's a vague dullness to my life that I usually can't put my finger on. It's like listening to the noise of my car for so long that I don't even hear it any longer. And since nothing is outwardly wrong and I seem to be doing fine on my own, I'm not aware of how desperately I need God.

However, like being oblivious to the danger of driving around with only one bolt holding my engine to the block, it's exactly when I think I can do fine on autopilot that I'm most susceptible to tumbling headfirst into sin. Sometimes it's not even the obvious "deadly" sins, but rather the subtle, soul-stealing, joy-robbing sin of self: self-reliance, self-dependence, self-sufficiency, and self-righteousness. When I'm trusting in myself, I'm essentially turning my back on God. Without meaning to or realizing it, I am in essence waving my fist in his face and declaring myself, the creature, greater than he, the Creator.

That's when I need God's help most. I need help to repent of my drifting and help to find my way back to dependence on his grace, and his grace alone, for my very next breath and heartbeat.

A line in a favorite hymn "Come, Thou Fount of Every Blessing" goes like this:

> O to grace how great a debtor,
> daily I'm constrained to be.
> Let Thy goodness, like a fetter,
> bind my wandering heart to Thee.

Prone to wander, I, too, need God's help to keep my heart bound to him. Without it, I cannot do anything. I cannot be kind, I cannot be generous, I cannot be patient or loving or care about anyone other than myself.

Unless God helps me, unless he is my help, I am without help and without hope.

GRABBING ONTO THE ROCK

The story of Hannah includes two of her prayers, polar opposites of each other. Her first prayer focused on her circumstances. She had been dwelling on what she did not have and desperately wanted. That is the human condition; we all pray similar prayers, and that's okay. The Bible tells us to pray about everything (Philippians 4:6).

Even Jesus, in a moment of unbearable humanity, prayed to have his circumstances altered. He prayed that he might bypass the cross and forgo suffering the Father's wrath. However, his ultimate prayer was one of surrender: "Yet not my will, but yours be done" (Luke 22:42). When he prayed, the Father sent angels to strengthen him. He came to his Son's rescue — not to deliver him from his situation but to comfort and strengthen him in it.

Sometimes we pray for help and deliverance, and God leaves us where we are. He says, "My grace is sufficient for you," and it is. Sometimes, however, he gives us the very thing we've asked for.

Hannah conceived and bore a son! Her plea for help was transformed into a song of praise. Even more amazing, once the child was weaned, she took him back to the tabernacle in Shiloh where she had wept bitterly and God had met her, and she left him there in the care of Eli, the priest. She gave back to God the very child she had begged him for, as she had vowed.

Then she prayed: "My heart rejoices in the LORD. . . . There is no one holy like the LORD; there is no one besides you; there is no Rock like our God" (1 Samuel 2:1–2).

After that, the Lord graciously granted Hannah three more sons and two daughters. Meanwhile, her firstborn, Samuel, "grew up in the presence of the LORD" (1 Samuel 2:21).

When Hannah had nowhere else to turn, she turned to the Rock of Ages, the God of all help and comfort and the One who holds life in his hand. Because she knew her helplessness and sought God, she was helped.

In our modern culture, we often despise our helplessness. We'd much rather be self-sufficient. It's the American way. But we were born helpless and created to be dependent.

The truth is, only the helpless can truly know the awesome rescuing power of the Almighty. Only those who cry out in dependence can know the loving dependability of the Father and the security of the Rock.

As you consider your own life, how have you despised your helplessness? We miss out on so much when we seek help in ourselves. Praise God that he forgives all those who ask for forgiveness and then graciously gives us plenty of opportunities to need his help! O may we learn from Hannah, fall on our knees, and ask.

Father,

I confess that I am often more like self-sufficient, take-control Sarah than God-dependent Hannah, and I know that grieves your heart. All the "self" words like "self-reliant" and "self-dependent," "self-sustaining" and "self-righteous" also too often describe my thinking when faced with troubles and trials.

The truth is, many times I can help myself, but when I do, I miss out on so much by not coming to you first for help. (Not to mention the mess I make by trying to do things myself!) Your help is far greater than anything I can conceive of. Without it, I would miss out on miracles and blessings and the sheer awe of watching you at work.

Create in me a greater dependence on you. I need your help to even know that I need it! There truly is no one holy like you. Help me, Lord, for you are my Rock, and apart from you, I am helpless, hopeless, and lost.

In your name, I pray. Amen.

Digging Deeper

Think: How have you tried to help yourself out of a trial, only to make things worse? How have you seen God's help when you've cried out to him?

Study: Psalm 46

Apply: How did God help Hannah? Read her story in 1 Samuel 1–2. In prayer, ask God to help you, believing that he can and will.

Consider: Hannah expected God to look on her and to remember her. He will do the same for all who belong to him.

Reflect: "I have been driven many times to my knees by the overwhelming conviction that I had nowhere else to go."–Martin Luther

THE PRAYER OF ESTHER
She Prayed with Courage

If I perish, I perish.

Esther 4:16

On March 23, 2003, nineteen-year-old Army Pfc. Jessica Lynch followed a wrong turn in the Iraqi desert and wound up as a P.O.W. in a hospital in Nasiriyah. This pretty blonde-haired young woman from Palestine, West Virginia, had wanted to be a schoolteacher but couldn't afford the college tuition, so she joined the military to finance her education. She chose a job as a supply clerk. A nice job for a nice girl.

She hadn't planned on a war breaking out.

During her ordeal she suffered broken and fractured bones and went more than a week without food.

On April 1, after receiving a tip from an Iraqi lawyer who had witnessed Lynch in the hospital being slapped by an Iraqi man clad in black, a team of Navy SEALs, Marine commandos, Air Force pilots, and Army Rangers risked their lives to save this one young woman.

They found her lying on a hospital bed, peering out from under a sheet, afraid. In the days following her dramatic rescue, her story of bravery and courage flooded the news media. The truth is, she just happened to be in the right place at the right time to be on the receiving end of others' acts of courage and bravery.

In many ways, Jessica Lynch's story is our story. Not many of us are fearless warriors. We just go about our lives doing what we do until one day we wind up in a situation where we're called upon to be courageous. That's when we discover that true courage is not necessarily charging ahead without fear. Instead, it's moving forward, or sometimes standing firm, in spite of knee-knocking, heart-pounding fear — and trusting God for the outcome.

CONFESSIONS OF A BEAUTY QUEEN

About 2,500 years before Jessica Lynch became an American media star during the Iraqi war, another young girl was about to become her own people's courageous darling.

"Pretty," "vivacious," "a sweet spirit," "winning personality" — that's what some of the judges wrote on their tally sheets during the Miss Persia Beauty Pageant. Before that, however, King Xerxes, ruler over 127 provinces from India to the Nile River, had given a grand banquet to display his power and majesty to all his military leaders and the princes and nobles of his provinces. At the same time, Queen Vashti, his wife, gave a banquet for all the women in the palace.

As the men ate and drank, Xerxes decided he would show off his beautiful wife to his guests and summoned her with a royal command.

"Tell my husband I'm busy," she replied.

This made Xerxes furious. Then, after consulting with his legal experts, he had Vashti banished from the kingdom "so all the women [throughout the kingdom] will respect their husbands, from the least to the greatest" (Esther 1;20).

Once his anger died down, Xerxes decided he needed another young, pretty wife and inaugurated a Miss Persia Beauty Pageant, with himself as the grand prize. The word went out into all the provinces, and beautiful wanna-be queens entered the pageant in droves.

Esther, a Jewish orphan who lived with her uncle Mordecai, was among the contestants. When she arrived at the citadel of Susa, she was put under the care of Hegai, the harem keeper. Immediately, Esther won his favor and was assigned seven maids to assist her during the twelve-month prepageant beauty treatments.

When it came her turn to visit the king for judging, she won his favor as well. After that, he crowned her his queen and sent all the other contestants away.

Haman the Horrible

Meanwhile, Uncle Mordecai happened to overhear a plot to assassinate the king. He told Esther, who told Xerxes, who wrote Mordecai's name down in his royal record book.

Now, the king had a royal official named Haman, who thought of himself more highly than he ought, because everyone was required to bow down to him. However, Mordecai, a Jew, refused. This infuriated Haman, who devised a plan to kill not only Mordecai, but the entire Jewish people.

By his cunning, Haman convinced the king to sign an edict decreeing that the Jews should die: young, old, women, and children, all in one day.

When Mordecai heard about it, he tore his clothes in anguish and wept bitterly with the rest of his people. After Esther's servants told the queen the news, she sent word to her uncle that she would, of course, speak to the king to see if he would change his edict: *Dear Uncle, I haven't seen the king in more than a month. To just barge in uninvited is a capital offense. I could lose my life.*

Mordecai replied: *My sweet niece. Don't think that because you are in the king's house that you will be the only Jew to escape. If you do nothing, relief and deliverance for the Jews will come from somewhere else, but you and your father's family will perish. Besides, who knows? God may have appointed you queen for just such a time as this.*

Esther sent word for Mordecai to gather the Jews in Susa together to fast and pray, and she would do the same. *I will go to the king, even though it is against the law. And if I perish, I perish.* (Esther 1–4)

TWINKLE, TWINKLE, LITTLE STAR

Although you and I may never wind up as P.O.W.s or become queens faced with risking our lives on behalf of a nation, every one of us will find ourselves in situations where we need courage. Most of the time, we're called to be lights in the darkness, right where we are, which takes its own kind of courage — not the courage needed by a soldier in a tank, barreling across the desert. Rather, we need the courage to remain "blameless and pure, children of God without fault in a crooked and depraved generation" (Philippians 2:15). We are to "shine like stars in the universe as [we] hold out the word of life" (2:15–16).

That's not always easy.

- Your boss asks you to "adjust" the books while she "borrows" company inventory.
- Your child brings home an assignment that involves the study of witchcraft, spells, and omens.
- You're single and lonely, and there aren't any decent single Christian men asking you out. But a nice guy at work has started paying attention to you. He's not a Christian, but . . .
- While at a party the conversation turns to the topic of religion. The consensus of the group is: Only brain-dead morons believe the Bible.
- You and your husband were both unbelievers when you got married, but now you're a Christian and your husband isn't. He wants his "old" wife back — Jesus-free, or else.

We all want to shine for Jesus and be lights in the darkness, but often it's a long way between wanting to and doing it, especially when the darkness looms large and our light is puny and weak. The pull to compromise is great.

In North America, we don't need courage to bear up under beatings and imprisonment for our faith. We need courage to step out of the gray, to turn off *The Jerry Springer Show*, to be the only mom who won't let her teenager go to a coed slumber party. We need courage

> *Although you and I may never wind up as P.O.W.s or become queens faced with risking our lives on behalf of a nation, every one of us will find ourselves in situations where we need courage.*

to not join in the gossip, to not go into debt, to be the only one in the family to follow Jesus.

We don't want to make waves. We want to avoid conflict. We want peace.

In his book, *No More Mr. Nice Guy*, Steve Brown writes about a "strange paradox" that he has discovered. He writes, "When I am too frightened to make waves for Christ, when I have chosen to go over in a corner and avoid conflict and problems, when I have chosen to take the easy way out, and when I have chosen to allow my faith to be insipid, I find that my anxiety level rises."

He goes on to say, "That which I think will lessen my worry and anxiety does just the opposite. However . . . when I stand, God stands with me."

On the one hand, whenever I've tried to compromise, I, too, have ended up even more anxious than if I had done what I knew I should do. On the other hand, in those times when I've taken a stand, even though I've been afraid, God has given me the courage I have needed to do the right thing, even without knowing the outcome beforehand.

When I first came to faith in Christ, I was the only born-again Christian in our family. To be honest, I was a bit overbearing and obnoxious about my faith and turned a few family members off. And because my faith became a divisive issue, especially between me and my husband, I considered bailing out — not of the marriage, but of the faith.

My insides churned as I wrestled with God over my predicament. Jesus had called me out of the darkness and into his light and then called me to shine for him. Yet, I wanted to please everyone I loved, and I certainly didn't want to make waves. Above all else, I hate conflict of any kind, and especially conflict in which I'm the reason.

So, I had made a decision: I would go back to the way things were. I was afraid of facing a future filled with conflict and turmoil and afraid my whole family would turn against me, including my husband.

One night Barry and I went out for Chinese food. It had been a particularly stressful day between us, and I desperately needed God to give me courage to go forward. That's when he sent his encouragement in a fortune cookie: "Have faith," it said on the little slip of paper.

Those two words were all I needed to go ahead with the hardest decision I had ever faced up to that time.

I was still afraid, but when I decided to stand firm and not run away, God stepped down from heaven and stood with me. More than twenty-five years later, I've never looked back because God has never left my side. As a result, I'm no longer the only Christian in my family, and God has used my life, my words, and my pen to bring others into his kingdom. Mordecai had reminded Esther: "Who knows but that you have come to royal position for such a time as this?" (Esther 4:14).

Likewise, the Lord poses that same question to each of his children whom he places in difficult and uncomfortable situations. Who knows but that you are (in this marriage, stricken with this illness, employed in this company, in a relationship with this in-law) as an emissary for him? His person for his purpose. Is there no greater calling?

> *Who knows but that you are (in this marriage, stricken with this illness, employed in this company, in a relationship with this in-law) as an emissary for him?*

When the Going Gets Tough . . .
Fall on Your Knees!

Esther was faced with a dilemma. As a Jew, she was among the ones condemned to die, and the day was fast approaching. Her only hope of saving her own life and that of her people was to petition the king. However, if her unannounced visit proved to be an annoyance to the king, she would lose her life. As she saw it, she faced a lose-lose situation unless she caught the king on a good day, and he extended the golden scepter to her.

Because life and death and the hearts of kings are in God's hands, Esther's first response to her desperate plight was to fast and pray and seek God's face. She prayed for herself, and she prayed for her people. Not as a last resort, but as a first resort. As Christians, the two greatest offensive and defensive weapons we have been given are the Word of God and prayer. In both, we find strength and courage sufficient for any task or trial God calls us to face.

We have also been given a support system, the local church. It's there we find like-minded believers who lift us up when we fall and steady us when we're weak and afraid. As a family, we cry together, laugh together — and pray together.

We pray with and for one another.

Esther understood the power that is derived from believers gathering together to pray. Likewise, God's people throughout the ages have always gathered for corporate prayer. Prayer binds us to one another and to the Father. Alone, we are afraid, but together, we're made strong.

On the third day of her fast, with her heart pounding from fear, Esther put on her royal robes and stood in front of the king's hall. When Xerxes saw Queen Esther, he smiled and held out his gold scepter, the sign that she could approach the throne. She had already approached God's throne, and he had encouraged her to go forward with her request to the king.

"Would you and Haman be my guests at a banquet tonight?" she asked.

The men came, they ate, they drank, they had a great time. Esther invited them back the following night as well, which put Haman in high spirits. The queen had invited him to her banquet — twice! — and no one else, he had boasted to his wife. But his good mood soured when he thought of Mordecai and his refusal to show Haman honor. "He's a real pain in my side, and he's spoiling all my fun!" he complained.

That's when his wife suggested he build a gallows to have Mordecai hanged.

Meanwhile, that night the king couldn't sleep and opened up the chronicles of his reign. As he read, he noticed the entry of the time Mordecai alerted him to the assassination plot.

"How have we rewarded him for this?" he asked his servant.

"We haven't done anything, sir."

Just then, Haman stopped by to see about having Mordecai hanged.

"Haman, what do you think should be done for a man the king delights to honor?" Xerxes asked.

Thinking the king meant him, Haman suggested a royal parade.

"Great idea! Take care of it for me; the parade's for Mordecai," said the king.

Haman did as the king commanded, even though it further fueled his hatred for Mordecai. However, he swallowed his anger in time to attend the queen's banquet, arriving in time to hear Esther's request of the king: "Please spare my life and that of my people." Then she revealed the king's own edict to have the Jews annihilated.

"Who's behind this?" the king demanded. When he learned it was Haman, he left in a rage. Then, in an attempt to beg Esther to spare his life, Haman fell on her, which the king saw and mistook for Haman trying to molest the queen. Haman ended up hanging on the very gallows he had erected for Mordecai.

In the end, Esther and her people were spared through another of the king's edicts, allowing the Jews to defend themselves. When the day of their scheduled annihilation came, they ended up slaughtering their enemies.

FROM BEAUTY QUEEN TO NATIONAL HERO

The story of Esther is the story of what God can do through an ordinary life. Esther started out wanting to win a beauty contest and ended up saving her nation from destruction. In between is where the real story is: that God chooses and uses ordinary people who are mostly afraid, hidden under their covers, and who don't always know what to do. But in their fear, through their prayers and petitions, God draws close. And because he goes with them, with you, and with me, even the most fearful and the most cowardly are made strong.

It's also the story of how God can use one woman and her friends down on their knees to change the course of a nation with their prayers.

My great God,
Here I am in the middle — in the middle of family, work, community. I'm in the middle of where you have

placed me to be a light in the darkness, to shine for you as I hold out your words of life.

My life may not be in danger, may not ever be in danger, but I still need courage to do what you have called me to do and to be who you have created me to be . . . right here in the middle, "for such a time as this."

I thank you that you meet me, walk with me, and stand with me as I stand for you. Thank you for your Holy Spirit, who gives me comfort and courage — for your Spirit, who empowers me.

"With your help I can advance against a troop; with my God I can scale a wall" (Psalm 18:29). Thank you, too, for the weapons of prayer and your powerful, mighty Word. In them — in you — I take refuge and find strength to stand, right here in the middle.

In your name, Jesus, I pray, Amen.

DIGGING DEEPER

Think: What situation are you in the middle of that you need courage to make it through?

Study: Ephesians 6:10–20

Apply: Each day, in prayer, "dress" yourself in God's armor as found in Ephesians 6, paying attention to how each piece can equip you for your battle.

Consider: Esther's most heroic deed was praying for her nation and trusting God for her future.

Reflect: "Courage is fear holding on a minute longer." –Gen. George S. Patton

THE PRAYER OF THE CANAANITE WOMAN
She Prayed for Mercy

Lord, Son of David, have mercy on me!
Matthew 15:22

In our family, my younger daughter, Laura, is known as "the baby Mom begged God for." My husband has often reminded me of that over the years, such as the time when she transformed the kitchen into a Barbie-theme water park, flooding the counters as Barbie careened down cookie-pan slides, or when she hid live "snail farms" under her bed. On another occasion she came home with her nose pierced and brought over friends with Skittles-colored hair and pointy objects sticking out of their lips.

Even so, she was and still is worth "begging" God for. With more than six years between my two daughters, I didn't think I would ever have a second child!

Laura has always had a heart of mercy as well as a fondness for the mischievous. She is bold and opinionated and the center of attention wherever she goes. So, when depression hit her several years ago shortly after her high school graduation, it took everyone who knew her by surprise. Unable to lift herself from our overstuffed black couch, she seemed to disappear into it, her black mood swallowed by the black sofa. She wouldn't — in fact, couldn't — eat or sleep. She couldn't find a reason to live. All she could do was cry.

Never having experienced depression myself, I could not relate to how she felt, nor did I know how to help her. All I knew was that the baby I begged God for, the one who had once driven me crazy with her relentless campaigns for eyebrow piercings and tattoos, the one who once could make me laugh until I cried and cry until I laughed, the one for whom I would gladly die, had sunk into a dark pit — and there was nothing I could do to pull her out. All I could do was to plead to God on her behalf for mercy.

"LORD, SON OF DAVID, HAVE MERCY ON ME!"

There was once another mother and another daughter. The gospel of Mark says she was a "little" daughter (Mark 7:25), but no matter what a child's age, to a mother, she's always your baby.

This mother, whose name we do not know, was a Gentile, a Canaanite, born in Syrian Phoenicia. The Canaanites had been foes of the Israelites since the days of Abraham and had no part in the covenant that God had made with his people.

Even so, this mother only knew that her child suffered from demon possession and that a man named Jesus had been traveling the region of Tyre and Sidon, healing the sick, raising the dead, and freeing those in bondage. He ate with sinners and touched lepers. Maybe he would touch her child, too.

I know I'm not a Jew, she may have thought, *and I am not worthy to even walk in this man's shadow. But this is my baby, and*

I don't know how to help her. This Jesus may be my only hope. I've heard that he is kind and that he loves the little ones. Perhaps he will overlook that I am a Canaanite and take pity on me.

Determination and desperation drove her to seek Jesus as she made her way through the crowds that pressed in around the traveling rabbi, this man of God. He was her last hope. He was her only hope.

When there's nothing else, there's mercy.

Through the dust and through her tears, ignoring the scorn of the disciples and the curses hurled at her from some of those who surrounded Jesus, she cried out, "Lord, Son of David, have mercy on me! My daughter is suffering terribly from demon-possession."

From a mother's lips to God's ears: "Please, have mercy!"

LORD, PLEASE SEND AN ANGEL!

Like the Canaanite woman, I, too, have cried out to the Lord for mercy: for myself as a mother and mercy for my daughter as well. Several years prior to her depression, Laura had drifted from the profession of faith she had made as a little girl and had lost her joy in being God's child.

Her language coarsened; her grades dropped. She explored other religious ideas and then settled on no religion. Fashion-wise, she went from "grunge" to "Goth," and she brought music into our house with lyrics that went beyond blasphemy.

That's when a battle ensued — not so much between the two of us, although as mother and daughter we exchanged many daggered, wounding words. During that time I knew that the battle was spiritual, that my wrestling with my daughter was essentially a fight for her soul.

After a week or so of battling with her and agonizing within myself — I couldn't eat; I couldn't think; all I could do was cry and pray — one afternoon I was drawn to her room while she was away at school. As I stood in the center, with a power I had never felt before or since, I commanded an evil presence, "In the name of Jesus, get out of my house and leave my daughter alone!"

I battled this presence for a while and even called a nearby pastor-friend to come over and help me pray. Eventually, the presence left, and when it did, the Spirit of God rushed in and filled my daughter's room and flooded my soul as well. Later, when my daughter came home from school and I told her what had happened, her eyes grew wide.

"I thought it was my imagination, but I've felt something scary in my room," she told me. After that, she didn't even put up a fight when I told her we needed to throw out the music that denigrated the name and character of Jesus. I had allowed evil into our house, but God showed both of us his mercy and removed it.

My daughter's depression, however, was different. It seemed to come from nowhere and sucker-punched her when she wasn't looking. After she spent about a month on the couch, a friend of hers from out of state invited her for a visit. I thought it would do her good and encouraged her to go.

One night I called to see how she was doing. Her friend's father answered the phone and said they had gone to a concert. I felt sick to my stomach when he told me the name of the band they went to hear. It was the same one whose music just two years earlier had brought an evil spirit into her room. Knowing her state of mind, I didn't know what she might have inadvertently opened herself to. I dropped to my knees and prayed, "Lord, in your great mercy, please send an angel to go get my daughter!" Looking back, I don't know why I prayed that. At the time it was simply what sprang from my lips.

The next day, when I picked her up from the airport, I asked about the concert.

"It was the weirdest thing," she said. "Standing right next to me the whole time was a guy in a bright yellow shirt that had JESUS on it. He just stood there, not doing anything." She shook her head. "Who goes to a concert in a yellow Jesus shirt?" she asked.

An angel goes, I thought.

After she had come home from visiting her friend, I noticed her mood had begun to lift. Even before her trip, she had been seeing a doctor for regular counseling, which helped her understand that depression was a physiological condition. Although she refused to take the medication prescribed for her, God intervened with his mercy and brought her out of her despair.

> *I didn't know what she might have inadvertently opened herself to. I dropped to my knees and prayed, "Lord, in your great mercy, please send an angel to go get my daughter!"*

Because our God is rich in mercy, he hears the cries for mercy from mothers like me and like the Canaanite woman, mothers who don't know where else to turn. He hears the cries from those who deserve his judgment and extends his mercy instead. Not because he has to, but always, only, because he wants to.

MERCY FOR THE LEAST DESERVING — MERCY FOR *ME*

When the Canaanite woman came to Jesus, pleading on behalf of her daughter, he didn't acknowledge her at first. Then he led her into an unusual conversation, which, on the surface, appears abrupt and almost unkind but was more likely an object lesson for his mercy- and faith-deficient disciples. Jesus told her, "I was sent only to the lost sheep of Israel" (Matthew 15:24).

The woman knelt before him and begged again, "Lord, help me!"

Jesus replied, "It is not right to take the children's bread and toss it to their dogs."

Not letting that deter her from seeking deliverance and restoration for her daughter, she told him, "Yes, Lord . . . but even the dogs eat the crumbs that fall from their masters' table."

Jesus answered, "Woman, you have great faith! Your request is granted" (Matthew 15:27–28).

The Lord didn't need his arm twisted to get him to change his mind and extend mercy. He knew all along what he would do. That's because mercy is at the center of God's heart. The psalmists and the prophets called his mercy "great." It's vast, unending, and new every morning. It's the response of a benevolent king toward a needy people. Jesus responded to this woman's plea for mercy because he *is* mercy.

We plead for mercy on others' behalf from a heart of helpless compassion. *Please, God, take pity on my child!*

Like asking for help, pleading for mercy is an instinctual prayer. Anyone who has ever had a big brother who likes to give a little sister a "hurts, don't it" (punching on the arm) understands pleading for mercy.

Evangelist Luis Palau tells the story of a mother who once approached Napoleon seeking a pardon for her son. The emperor reminded her that justice for her son's crimes demanded death.

"But I don't ask for justice," the mother replied. "I plead for mercy."

"But your son does not deserve mercy," Napoleon said.

The woman cried, "Sir, it would not be mercy if he deserved it, and mercy is all I ask for."

Mercy granted, the emperor spared the woman's son.

The Bible offers many examples of God's mercy granted to those who cried out for it: a man pleading for mercy for his demon-possessed son, another distraught father seeking mercy for a dying daughter, a blind man begging for mercy that he might see.

Solomon prayed for mercy on behalf of the Israelites at the dedication of the temple in Jerusalem. Nehemiah prayed and recounted how God had been merciful to his people in the past. The Canaanite woman pleaded for mercy for her daughter and received it; the girl was delivered from her demons. Likewise, I pleaded for mercy for my daughter and received it.

Oh, how great is the mercy of God!

MERCY CAME RUNNING

A prayer for mercy begins with an acknowledgment of utter undeserving. "The Lord our God is merciful and forgiving, even though we have rebelled against him," writes Daniel in Daniel 9:9. Not simply that I come asking with empty hands, but with soiled and bloody hands. I come agreeing that I deserve judgment and knowing that if I receive it, I will have received it fairly and therefore have no basis for complaint or protest. I am entitled to nothing other than punishment.

The Canaanite woman gave no reason or justification for her plea, just a desperate, heartfelt, "Lord, Son of David, have mercy on me!" Although she was a Canaanite, she called Jesus "Lord" and acknowledged him as "Son of David," the promised Redeemer of Israel. Not even the religious Jews called him that.

Isn't it ironic that it's often the most religious who miss God's mercy? That shows that it depends solely on God. How great is his mercy!

Jesus told a story illustrating the mercy of God (see Luke 15:11–31). There was a son who, in essence, told his father he wished him dead and demanded his share of his inheritance. Then he took off and squandered it all on riotous living. If he had done it today, he might have gone to Atlanta, Boston, Las Vegas, or New York City and lived on the streets shooting himself up with drugs and buying prostitutes for the night.

But then when the money ran out, when he had to resort to prostituting himself to support his habit and scrounge for food in the trash bins behind restaurants, when he had to sleep with one eye open to keep from being beaten, he began thinking about mercy. To this young man, *mercy* had been just another religious word like *grace* or *forgiveness* that he had heard in church growing up but didn't care two bits about — until then.

> To this young man, mercy *had been just another religious word like* grace *or* forgiveness *that he had heard in church growing up but didn't care two bits about — until then.*

It started with a longing for home and the realization that he could never be welcomed back as a son — not after the hurtful things he'd said to his father, not after the shameful things he had done. All he could hope for was mercy. A job as a hired hand, maybe a pile of straw to sleep on and left-overs to eat.

I'm so sorry, Dad, he rehearsed. *I'd make it up to you if I could, but I have nothing; I am nothing, and I know I've hurt you.*

As the young man headed for home, mercy ran to greet him. When he was still a long way off, his father, who had been waiting and watching, praying and begging God, "Have mercy on my son!" saw him in the distance. The father hiked up his robes and ran toward his son, running faster than he ever thought possible. Upon seeing his son's brokenness and con-trition, forgiveness and mercy leaped from within his being, and he hugged and kissed the son he had given up for dead.

"Dad, if you only knew what I've done," he said, back-ing away from his father's embrace, too ashamed to look him in the eye. "I've sinned against God and against you. I don't deserve your forgiveness." As he spoke, he hoped against hope and silently pleaded for mercy. Then, lifting his eyes to his father, he not only received mercy, he received grace.

Mercy is Napoleon letting a condemned man go free. Mercy is the father allowing the son to work in the field in repayment of the squandered inheritance. Grace, however, would be Napoleon adopting the young man. Grace is the father throwing a homecoming party for his son. It's the father wiping the son's slate clean and restoring him to the position of beloved child, redecorating his bedroom, and buying him a car. Grace is guilt erased, an "unrepayable" debt satisfied, a celebration over the lost being found. It's a party in honor of the least deserving.

Praying — and Playing — at the Father's Feet

In what areas of your life do you need mercy? Whether for yourself or someone else, every child of God can "approach the throne of grace with confidence" to "receive mercy and find grace to help ... in ... time of need" (Hebrews 4:16). Picture JFK Jr. as a toddler playing underneath the president's desk, confident that he won't be turned away by the most powerful man in the world, his father. We who are God's children have that same confidence whenever we go to our Father. He won't turn us away either. His nature is mercy, his heart is grace, his essence is love. We need not fear him.

Although the Canaanite woman was outside the covenant relationship God had with his people, she went to Jesus for mercy. She believed he could help her, hoped that he would, and then rejoiced when he did.

The nineteenth-century hymn writer Henry Lyte wrote these words:

> Father-like, he tends and spares us;
> well our feeble frame he knows;
> in his hands he gently bears us,
> rescues us from all our foes.

Our God is King, but he is also Father. He is Sovereign, yet he is "Dad."

Because of that, we who are his can come to his throne with dirty, outstretched hands and walk away reclaimed, restored, rejoicing.

Lord,

Of all your wonderful attributes, I think I love your mercy best. I can't always comprehend love or grace, but mercy is something I can grasp. Have mercy on me, a sinner!

As I look to the cross and am aware of my guilt, it's mercy that I cry for. It's mercy that you offer. Deserving your wrath, I receive your kindness. You tell me I'm forgiven, then call me your child. When I run from you, you go and get me, not to punish me, but to show me mercy. Have mercy on me, a sinner!

My sin and my need are great, but your mercy is so much greater. For myself, for others, I ask for mercy — not expecting, not demanding it, but hoping. Lord, be merciful to me, a sinner!

In Jesus' name, Amen.

DIGGING DEEPER

Think: When was the last time you asked God for mercy? How did he answer your prayer?

Study: Psalm 31

Apply: We often pray, "God, be merciful to me, a sinner." Offer to the Lord a prayer of thanksgiving for all the ways he has shown you mercy.

Consider: No one *deserves* mercy, which makes it all the more precious a gift.

Reflect: "Our prayer and God's mercy are like two buckets in a well; while the one ascends, the other descends." —Mark Hopkins

THE PRAYER OF THE WOMAN WHO NEEDED HEALING

She Prayed with Faith

If I just touch his clothes, I will be healed.
Mark 5:28

Faceless, nameless, an outcast for twelve years, the woman pulled her wrap tightly around her thin shoulders. Even though it was spring, she shivered. She was cold; she was always cold. She could barely recall the days when she was robust, even on the plump side. But now, after twelve years of continual bleeding, the kind that made a woman ritually unclean, she hardly recognized her own taut, drawn reflection. So weak, so tired.

So lonely.

According to Mosaic law, a woman's period or any type of bleeding or discharge made her "unclean." Even though such occurrences are natural, for the Jews, anything the law deemed "unclean" was to be a reminder of their sinfulness in contrast to the holiness of God.

Therefore, anything a woman sat on, any bed she slept in, anyone she touched or who touched her, even accidentally, also became ritually unclean. To be made "clean" again, the woman had to wait until her bleeding stopped for seven days. On the eighth day, she was required to go through a ritual of purification by bringing doves or pigeons as a sin and a burnt offering to the priest for sacrifice. Only then could she touch or be touched by others (see Leviticus 15:19–31).

But because her bleeding had never ceased, this nameless, hopeless woman had long given up any thought of marriage or children.

As she carefully made her way through the crowded Jerusalem streets, she averted her eyes from those around her. Not that anyone ever really saw her. She often wondered if her bleeding had made her invisible. Maybe no one saw her because she stayed hidden in the shadows, afraid.

Normally, she didn't venture out in a crowd; she didn't dare risk contaminating anyone. But she had heard about the healing rabbi who was said to have compassion on women. She had spent her every last cent going from doctor to doctor, but not one of them could heal her. Instead of getting better, she only grew worse.

Now, out of money, out of strength, out of ideas, and out of hope, this faceless, nameless woman set out to find the Healer.

"WHO TOUCHED ME?"

Although there wasn't a logical explanation, somehow she knew that the Healer would know her name. She had learned his name was Jesus. *Jesus, the one who had compassion on the desperate and needy. The one who just might have compassion on me,* she thought.

Just then she saw him. She held her breath and prayed, "If I could just touch his clothes, I know I will be healed!"

Then, reaching out her hand, stretching her faith farther than she ever dared before, risking being singled out and further ostracized because of her uncleanness, she brushed her fingertips against the hem of Jesus' cloak as he passed by. Immediately, her bleeding stopped, and she knew that she was finally freed from her suffering. For the first time in twelve years, she felt hopeful. She raised herself up and was about to turn and go when Jesus asked, "Who touched me?"

Fear stabbed her between her shoulder blades. Because she, an unclean woman, had touched the rabbi, she would be responsible for his uncleanness. She steeled herself for what was certain to come next — public humiliation and scorn. It was something she had become used to, but it hurt nonetheless.

"Who touched me?" Jesus had asked.

The disciples all shrugged. With so many people pressing in all around, it could have been anyone. "Someone touched me," Jesus said. "I know that power has gone out from me."

Jesus knew this was not an ordinary touch. This was a touch of faith, and it was faith that touched not just his garment but his heart.

He scanned the crowd and his gaze stopped at the thin woman who stood frozen in fear. As he drew closer to her, she fell at his feet trembling and spilled out her story. "Daughter," he said to her, "your faith has healed you. Go in peace" (Matthew 9:20–22; Mark 5:25–34; Luke 8:43–48).

HOW MUCH FAITH IS ENOUGH?

Spend enough time in Christian circles, and you're bound to hear conflicting ideas about the "prayer of faith." The New Testament writer James says, "The prayer offered in faith will make the sick person well" (James 5:15). However, does that mean every "prayer offered in faith" will make every sick person well, as some believe? If so, if I pray and the person is not made well, does that mean I didn't pray in faith? Or if I prayed in faith, maybe I didn't have enough faith? If that's true, how much is "enough" faith? And how do I get it?

If God is waiting for me to have enough faith before he will answer my prayer, that must mean the answer depends on me — on *my* faith. Taken to its logical conclusion, the "prayer of faith" is really a prayer of faith in my faith. If that's true, and if the answer to my prayer depends on my faith and God can't work without it, then that must mean I am greater than God.

> *Spend enough time in Christian circles, and you're bound to hear conflicting ideas about the "prayer of faith."*

But, if God is sovereign and almighty, which he is, and if he is the One who hears and answers all prayer, then the size and intensity of my faith isn't even an issue. Rather, the issue is the object of my faith: Christ and him alone. He is the One whom Scripture calls the "author and perfecter" of my faith. Therefore, any faith I have begins and ends with him.

WHERE FAITH BEGINS

Ask a dozen people to explain faith, and you will get a dozen answers. It's been described as "belief in the face of all contradictions" (Paul Tournier), "expecting from God what is beyond all expectation" (Andrew Murray), and "trusting God with the impossible" (Ruth Bell Graham).

One woman explained faith as standing on the edge of a precipice and stepping off, certain one of two things will happen: There will either be something solid to stand on or you will learn to fly.

The writer of Hebrews said faith is "being sure of what we hope for and certain of what we do not see" (Hebrews 11:1). It's Noah spending one hundred years building a boat in the desert in preparation for a flood even though it had never rained before. It's an old, decrepit, childless Abraham and Sarah setting up a nursery in anticipation of a baby promised to them by God. It's believing the impossible is more than possible and that God specializes in impossible situations.

It's a woman reaching out her hand as a last resort.

Jesus told the woman, "Your faith has healed you." Likewise, when the Canaanite woman begged Jesus for mercy for her demon-possessed daughter, he told her the same thing. "Woman, you have great faith! Your request is granted."

Another time, a Roman soldier approached Jesus on behalf of his paralyzed servant, asking only that Jesus say the word and his servant would be healed. Jesus commended the man for having faith greater than anyone else in Israel. Again, when a blind man begged to see and a leper begged to be healed, Jesus declared that it was their faith that healed them.

What kind of faith did they have in common? Not great and grand faith of visions and dreams and glorious possibilities. Instead, theirs was a faith borne of desperation, standing at the edge of a precipice. That's where all faith begins. *I have exhausted all my resources and my options. I've done all I could and nothing has worked. I have nowhere else to go except to God. I'm scared, but I'm going to take a step now ...*

FLYING LESSONS

I learned to "fly" when, two weeks after finding out that I was pregnant with my younger daughter, my husband lost his job and remained unemployed for an entire year. Without health insurance, without a regular income, without a guarantee that we would be able to pay our rent and/or car payment from month to month, or even buy food, I stood at the edge of the precipice. Life had been predictable up until then. But I had come to the edge, and I knew I had to take a leap.

I had tried desperately to solve our situation with logic and luck and government programs, but nothing panned out. So there I was, faced with two options: I could believe there was no God and everything was spinning out of control and I and my family were doomed, or I could believe that God had everything in his absolute control and he would take care of us.

Terrified that I just might have to learn to fly, by faith I jumped into the Father's arms. That's when I discovered that when there's nothing left to hold on to, faith holds out its hand believing that God's hand is already outstretched and waiting. And because he is faithful and rewards faith, his hand is always there.

As it turned out, for that entire year God met every one of our needs above and beyond anything we could have ever imagined. My husband found enough short-term jobs to pay most of our bills, and the rest were covered by a series of God-inspired gifts from mostly anonymous donors. God even miraculously covered the cost of delivering the baby through a serendipitous sixty-day Air Force National Guard tour of duty that my husband was chosen to take.

Would God have provided for us even if I hadn't put my faith in him? Of course. It's his nature to care for his own.

But if I hadn't, by faith, placed my impossible situation into his hands, I might have missed his personal touch on my behalf *as a direct answer to my prayer.*

True faith is an empty-handed expression of my humble and utter dependence on God alone. Its only requirements are an awareness of need and a repentance of trusting in anything or anyone other than God, including trusting in oneself. It contributes nothing, offering nothing *to* God, but gains everything, receiving everything *from* God.

That is the faith that pleases God and the faith that he rewards.

What Faith Isn't

Because faith is nebulous — by its very nature, it's something unseen — any discussion of the topic, especially as it pertains to prayer, is open to misconceptions and misunderstandings.

For one thing, faith isn't dependent on feelings. Several years ago my husband went through a time of depression. This was before Laura's depression, so neither he nor I recognized what was happening to him — to us. At first, I thought it was a midlife crisis. Maybe he stopped loving me. Maybe he was secretly taking drugs. I didn't know, and he wouldn't talk about what was going on. He acknowledged that something was wrong, but he refused to seek help. At that time, he worked out of town and didn't even come home for weeks at a time.

I didn't know from one day to the next if he would leave me for good, or even if he would take his own life. My emotions were all over the place as I waited and prayed. I cried daily, and some days I could barely keep myself focused on simple tasks.

Even so, if you would have asked me about the condition of my faith during that time, I would have said, "My faith is firm, although my feelings aren't." That's because my faith was not in my husband's condition improving, because I knew there are no such guarantees in this life. Instead, my faith was in knowing that God would give sufficient grace for whatever lay ahead. Feelings are fickle, but faith stands firm.

Barry came out of his depression slowly, without counseling or medication, although I had urged him to get help. I attribute his "healing" to a wonderful work of God, borne of the prayers of the people who love my husband. None of it had anything to do with my feelings, but everything to do with the faithfulness of God, the One in whom I place my faith.

Faith also isn't dependent on size or amount. How often have you heard someone say, "You just have to have more faith"? A man once brought his demon-possessed son to Jesus. The disciples had tried to drive out the evil spirit, but they could not. The man begged Jesus, "If you can do anything, take pity on us and help us."

Addressing his and the disciples' seeming lack of faith, Jesus replied, "'If you can'? . . . Everything is possible for him who believes" (Mark 9:23). Another time, when the disciples had asked Jesus to increase their faith, he told them that if all they had was faith as small as a mustard seed, they had all the faith they needed to move mountains (Matthew 17:20).

Upon hearing Jesus' words, the man with the demon-possessed son cried out, "I do believe; help me overcome my unbelief!" Even with only a small faith, the man received the answer to his prayer when Jesus cast out the evil spirit that had tormented his son from childhood. Even a mustard-seed-sized prayer that says, "Lord, I know you can, but I'm not sure you will," has the potential to change the course of history.

Finally, faith isn't dependent on the absence of doubt. Again, because faith is trusting in that which cannot be seen or touched, there's always the potential for doubt. The father of the demon-possessed son doubted ("Help me overcome my unbelief!"). So did Thomas the disciple, who, when the others announced that they had seen Jesus risen from death, said, "Unless I see the nail marks in his hands ... I will not believe it" (John 20:25).

> *Even a mustard-seed-sized prayer that says, "Lord, I know you can, but I'm not sure you will," has the potential to change the course of history.*

Instead of rebuking these men for their doubting ("Don't think — just believe!"), Jesus met them at their point of faith. Then he revealed himself as the One who is worthy of faith by casting out the evil spirit from the man's son and by showing Thomas his fatal wounds.

God always meets us where we are, accepting even our most doubt-filled prayers. However, he doesn't leave us there. He may let us see before we believe, but only to encourage and help us next time to believe before we see. That's the goal: the perfecting of our faith, so that every prayer we pray will be one of unwavering belief as we reach out to touch the hem of the Savior.

MOVING MOUNTAINS ON YOUR KNEES

Do you want to pray faith-filled prayers? Then go back to the moment in which you first believed, the moment you knew you had nothing to offer the God of grace and glory except your sin and your need. Go back to that tiny spark of faith mixed with doubt and fear, hope and desperation, and believe that that is all the faith you will ever need for God to move the tallest mountain in your life or to change the hardest heart — even your own.

Go back and believe that a prayer of faith doesn't depend on the prayer or the pray-er but solely on the One to whom we pray.

The One who loves us. The One who hears our cries of desperation. The One who, when one of his own reaches out, responds by saying, "Someone touched me."

When we've touched the heart of God, there's nothing that cannot be accomplished in our lives.

Father,

How many times have I come to you with my faithless prayers? Too often for me to count, that's how many. Does it grieve you when I say, "I know that you are able to do this, but I'm not sure if you will"? It grieves me to say it, but that's what I sometimes think. It's what I sometimes feel.

Yet . . .

What little faith I have, I am confident that it is all that I need and all that you require from me. For the faith that pleases you is my simple faith that believes I have no hope outside of you. So, I bring you my need, desperate to touch just the hem of your garment. I have no faith in my own faith; my faith is in you.

I believe, Lord! Help my unbelief. You are God — and I am yours.

In Jesus' name I pray. Amen.

DIGGING DEEPER

Think: What is your faith currently up against? How have you reached out to "touch the hem" of Jesus?

Study: Hebrews 11

Apply: As you think about your current situation, finish this sentence: "If I had faith, I would _____." In prayer, ask God to help you put your faith into action.

Consider: Faith is based on relationship and grows as my relationship with God grows.

Reflect: "Faith does not operate in the realm of the possible. There is no glory for God in that which is humanly possible. Faith begins where man's power ends."–George Müller

THE PRAYER OF SALOME
She Prayed with Boldness

Grant that one of these two sons of mine may sit at
your right and the other at your left in your kingdom.
Matthew 20:21

D*ear God,*
Since you wrote the Bible, you already know that it says I don't
have what I want because I haven't asked you, so now I'm asking. In
addition to love, joy, peace on earth, and so on, I want more money.
Not a lot, just enough so I don't have to think before I spend. I want
to lose twenty pounds by Friday without having to go without French
toast and cheesecake.

I want a smaller nose and a larger house — with self-cleaning
everything. I want to be able to take award-winning photographs,
write best-selling books, and dance without tripping.

While I'm asking, Lord, please arrange it so my children have
fulfilling careers with job security. Oh, and I still have one child who
wants to go away to college, so I'm asking you for the full tuition (in
advance) to the school of her choice, and a nice place for her to live,
preferably with a roommate who loves to clean up after people.

I want my children to have lives without struggles, yet they should have strong character. And strong faith, but don't let it be tested, Lord! Don't let them cry or doubt or question. Above all, I want them to be happy. In Jesus' name. Amen.

Be honest. Aren't your prayers like the one above? Maybe not the prayers you utter during your group Bible study prayer time or even the ones you whisper while alone in the shower, but the silent ones deep in your heart. They're the prayers that come from a heart tainted by original sin, borne of self. We want what we want when we want it, for ourselves, for our children. That's human nature.

And that's where God meets us.

JUST A NICE JEWISH MOTHER

Her boys, James and John, were nicknamed the "Sons of Thunder." Maybe they made a lot of noise around the house when they were younger. Maybe they played the Israelite version of touch football in the yard and bowled over all the other neighborhood boys. Maybe they were bold and brash, fearless men in the face of the often sudden and violent storms out on the Sea of Galilee as they cast their nets and pulled in their catch.

The Bible doesn't say how Salome was introduced to Jesus, but we know that her boys met him while in a boat preparing their nets. Jesus called to them from the beach and they dropped their nets, left their father in the boat with the hired men, and followed Jesus. Just like that.

In Yiddish, that took *chutzpah* to leave their father and the family fishing business. It takes *chutzpah* to risk everything to follow Jesus. Maybe they learned it from their mother. Maybe they were the ones to lead her to Jesus, knowing that she would be willing to risk too.

The Bible also doesn't say whether or not Salome's husband also followed Jesus, but she did. Despite the intense scrutiny of the Romans toward anyone associated with Jesus, she was among the women who waited at the cross as the Savior died and was one of the ones to go to his tomb on resurrection morning. That took *chutzpah*.

So did Salome's prayer request.

We meet Salome in Matthew 20. Jesus is on his way to Jerusalem for the last time. He takes his twelve disciples aside and tells them exactly what's going to happen, that he will be betrayed to the chief priests and teachers of the law in Jerusalem, who will condemn him to death. After that he will be turned over to the Gentiles to be mocked, flogged, and crucified, and on the third day he will be raised to life.

As Jesus speaks, Salome approaches him. Her sons are there too. Most likely, they have been listening to Jesus explain their Jerusalem itinerary. Somehow, they don't comprehend. They signal to their mother and mouth the words, "Ask him."

The gospel of Mark records the Zebedee brothers as already asking Jesus the same thing their mother is about to ask. Perhaps they went to her, laying out their plan. "You know, Mom," said one of them, "we've been with Jesus for three years now, and we've noticed that he's never refused a woman her request. So, we thought that if you asked him for us. . . ."

How could a mother refuse such a request from her darling boys? And what they want, to sit next to Jesus in his kingdom, well, don't they deserve it? Such good sons, these boys of mine. Of course Salome would ask Jesus. What mother wouldn't?

So, she approaches Jesus and kneels before him and says, "Jesus, could I ask a favor of you?"

First, the Good News . . .

Because Salome's request sounds opportunistic and self-promoting (or at least offspring-promoting), her story is often used as a negative example of what not to do and say when approaching the Son of God with a prayer request. However, there are several positive aspects of her request that we can learn from and follow.

First, Salome approached Jesus asking for a "favor." You ask favors of those in authority over you, of governors and princes and kings. You also ask favors of friends and family, people with whom you have a relationship.

Salome knew Jesus. He had been her sons' friend for three years. She cooked for him and had him over to her house. She followed him, listened to him, and learned from him. She felt comfortable in his presence and secure enough in his character to ask a favor of him as both one who was grand and great as well as one whom she knew personally. In drawing close to God, we find he draws close to us, which creates security. *I can ask a "favor" from the Almighty because I know he won't fry me on the spot for asking.*

Next, Salome was specific in her request. She didn't ask a generic "Please bless me and my kids," but instead told the Lord exactly what she wanted: "I want my boys to have a position of honor in your regime. Maybe one could be vice president in charge of defense and diplomacy and the other could head the kingdom ways and means department? Just so my boys are taken care of."

Salome had heard Jesus say, "Ask and it will be given to you," so she asked.

Jesus often asked people, "What do you want me to do for you?"

Some would answer, "I want to see." Others would seek him out and ask, "Lord, please heal my child," "Help our friend to walk." When we start with what we want, we often learn what it is we need. Jesus healed a paralyzed man, but not before telling him that his sins were forgiven. I might ask Jesus for a million dollars, but what I need is to know that God loves me and will always take care of me. Salome asked for what she wanted, and Jesus showed her that she needed to look beyond a kingdom on earth to a spiritual kingdom.

"WE WANT MEAT!"

In addition to being specific with her request, Salome dared to ask big. Not "Let my boys work in the palace kitchen," but "Make them kingdom generals." After all, Jesus told his disciples, "Ask . . . seek . . . knock." He said to pray, "Give us today our daily bread" (Matthew 6:11) and "My Father will give you whatever you ask in my name" (John 16:23).

However, even when we're specific, God doesn't always give us what we ask. As James the letter writer points out, we don't have what we want because we ask amiss; we ask with wrong motives. We pray for riches and fame and hot fudge sundaes or a body like Cindy Crawford's, "that [we] may spend what [we] get on [our] pleasures" (James 4:2–3).

Or, we ask for things that would thwart God's plan if answered the way we imagine they should be. Monica, the mother of the great fifth-century church father Augustine of Hippo, prayed long and hard for her wayward son. At one point she feared that her son would go to Rome, where he would fall further into sin, and she pleaded with God to keep her son from going. Despite the fervency of her prayers, Augustine went to

Rome anyway. While there he met Ambrose, who was instrumental in leading Augustine to faith in Christ.

We pray for silver, but God often gives us gold instead, said Martin Luther. We pray, "Please cure Joe's cancer," "Let Amy get into NYU," "Find Paul a job here in town so he won't have to move away." We pray boldly and specifically, but we pray for silver. Instead, God gives gold when Joe's cancer is not cured, but his faith is strengthened and his testimony touches his entire community. God gives gold when Amy is turned down by NYU, but learns the joy of giving when she stays home to attend community college and uses the money she saves to help support a friend who wants to go on the mission field. God gives gold when Paul finds a job a thousand miles away where he meets a struggling local pastor and helps him start a church.

It's not wrong to pray for "silver" if we leave the outcome to God's sovereignty. Besides, sometimes we don't know what to pray for. It is wrong, however, to "demand" our silver. In some instances, in demanding silver from God we receive rocks instead.

Just ask the Israelites. After God miraculously brought them out of slavery in Egypt, all they could do as they wandered in the desert was complain about the food — the manna that God had given them. "We want meat!" they demanded.

"You want meat? I'll give you meat," God said. So, they ate meat — and fell ill; some even died. That's the danger of demanding from God.

Although most of us aren't as bold as the Israelites to yell our demands, we do it in other ways. Our demands are polite, reverent, and religious as, through a misunderstanding or misinterpretation of Scripture, we try to hold God to promises he's never made. Without a full understanding of

Bible passages and promises in their context, we often run the risk of trying to force God's hand. It's one thing to use God's Word as a basis for prayer, but it's quite another to use it as a tool of manipulation.

Lord, you said, "Believe in the Lord Jesus, and you will be saved — you and your household." OK, I believe, so now you have to save my household or else you'll be a liar.

The problem is, that "promise" isn't a blanket promise for all believers; rather, it was part of a historical exchange between the apostle Paul and a Roman jailer when he was in a Philippi prison, after an

> *Our demands are polite, reverent, and religious as we try to hold God to promises he's never made.*

earthquake opened the prison doors and unlocked Paul's chains.

I still cringe when I think of my early years as a Christian and approaching God with that and other "promises" I pulled haphazardly out of the Bible. I'd pray, "You said I could ask anything in Jesus' name and I would receive it, so here's what I want." Mostly I prayed for noble things, such as my husband to accompany me to a church sweetheart dinner. I would call a bunch of friends and claim Jesus' words that "if two of you on earth agree about anything you ask for, it will be done for you by my Father in heaven" (Matthew 18:19). We would "agree," but often what I asked for wasn't "done" by the Father.

So, I'd go back to God, angry and frustrated. "You said!" I'd remind him. "You said if I asked, you said if two agree. . . . You said — and you lied!" And there I would be, the creature dressing down the Creator, the child telling the Father how to run the family.

The truth is, we are invited and encouraged by God to come to him boldly with our requests. But God is still God, and when we ask amiss, when we misuse the Scriptures to try and strong-arm the Almighty, even with humble, religious-sounding words, what we receive is correction — sometimes with a gentle rebuke, other times, as with the Israelites, with a bout of food poisoning from rancid meat.

Our Father knows best how to answer our requests, and as Sovereign Lord, he is still the One on the throne.

WHO'S ON FIRST?

One of the continuous threads throughout Scripture is that the last shall be first, the least are the ones who are great, and the greatest is the one who is servant to all. It's upside down and contrary. Although Salome had watched Jesus be a servant leader to his band of disciples, which included her sons, she didn't "get" it. Neither did her boys.

As she approached Jesus and made her request, he directed his reply, not to Salome, but to James and John. Maybe they had asked their mother to do the asking for them. *He'll say yes to you, Mom. He always says yes to women.*

"You don't know what you are asking," Jesus said to them. "Can you drink the cup I am going to drink?" (Matthew 20:22).

They answered, "Of course we can!"

Jesus told them that they would, indeed, drink from his cup of suffering. But as for being given a seat of kingdom honor, only the Father decides who sits where. Then he instructed all of the disciples in the upside-down ways of the kingdom: Whoever wants to be first must first serve. The humble shall be exalted, but those who exalt themselves will be humbled. With his answer, Jesus humbled the chest-thumping Sons of Thunder.

He did not, however, rebuke Salome for her asking, which is encouraging and comforting to those of us who pray. God is almighty, and he corrects those who err, but he's not like the terrifying Wizard of Oz, who tells people to leave his presence. As God, he is to be approached with trembling awe and reverent respect, but he is also a kindly King. He is a gentle Father who desires a relationship with us, his children.

God is almighty, and he corrects those who err, but he's not like the terrifying Wizard of Oz, who tells people to leave his presence.

Sometimes our prayers will be right on the mark. Sometimes they will be other-centered and kingdom-advancing. We'll ask boldly in Jesus' name and receive that which we've asked for. Sometimes, however, like Salome, we will ask amiss. We won't know how to pray or what to pray for. Our sin, which taints our vision, will cause us to pray for things that would end up destroying us.

Yet, God bids us to come and ask for what we want. To pray boldly, often, with fervency and gusto. To believe that he is "able to do immeasurably more than all we ask or imagine, according to his power that is at work within us" (Ephesians 3:20).

Is there something you want from God? Maybe you're not sure if what you want is in his will for you or if it would be "gold" for you. Go ahead and ask. The key is leaving the outcome of our requests up to the benevolent sovereignty of the One who sits on the throne. That way, we're never disappointed.

As we pray, we may not receive that answer we hope for, but we will always receive the answer that we need. And the answer is always, ultimately gold.

Father,

There's so much that I want: good health and long life, enough money and food, an air conditioner that always works in the summer and a car that works . . . always. I want smooth sailing and smooth skin — and happiness for my kids.

I know what I want, but I don't know what I need. How grateful I am that I can come to you with my dreams and even my outrageous wants, knowing that you will welcome me with delight, as your precious daughter.

I am confident that you will hear my prayer and will do that which is best for me. As for my list of wants, I know, too, that in time you will change my heart to conform my desires to yours.

Meanwhile, in all humility, yet with the boldness you said I can use, here is my request: _____. I leave it at your throne.

In Jesus' name I pray. Amen.

DIGGING DEEPER

Think: What are your wildest desires for yourself or your children?

Study: Luke 11:1–13; 1 John 5:14–15

Apply: Jesus told his followers to ask, seek, and knock in prayer. Using the above Scriptures as a guide, ask God for what you want in prayer, and then ask him to conform your wants to his.

Consider: Salome asked for what she thought was best for her children, but God gave them what he knew they needed.

Reflect: "Good prayers never come creeping home. I am sure I shall receive either what I ask, or what I should ask." –Joseph Hall

THE PRAYER OF THE "SINFUL" WOMAN
She Prayed with a Contrite Heart

> *For the sake of your name, O LORD,*
> *forgive my iniquity, though it is great.*
>
> Psalm 25:11

I learned to say my prayers as a little girl and could rattle off *"OurFatherwhichartinheavenhallowedbeThyname ..."* flawlessly in one breath, earning me the admiration of the other students in my Saturday morning catechism class and extra points from the teacher.

I got the chance to use my memorized prayers once a week, usually on Saturdays after catechism class, when I would wander into the church, dip my fingers in the holy water, tap my forehead, chest, and shoulders in a "sign of the cross," and genuflect before the altar. Then I would wait my turn to enter the confessional, shut the door, and confess my sins.

Our church was old and dark inside. Before I knew what a confessional was, I thought the dark wooden doors that lined the inner walls of the church were broom closets.

Before that, when I was about five, I thought they kept the devil behind those doors.

But even after I learned what a confessional was, I still didn't know what confession meant, at least not the "broken spirit and contrite heart" confession that God requires. Instead, when it came my turn, I would enter the confessional and tell the priest my sins: "I hit my brother twice; I harbored bad thoughts; I told three 'white' lies and one whopper."

Most of the time I made sins up just to have something to say.

Next, the priest would dole out "penance," usually a number of prayers to recite. Then, before I was allowed to leave the confessional, I was required to "make a good Act of Contrition." Again, another prayer to rattle off without thought of its words or meaning.

The prayer begins, "O my God, I am heartily sorry for having offended Thee." However, for the longest time I thought it went, "O my God, I am *partly* sorry. . . ."

To be honest, my version was closer to the truth of what was going on in my heart.

AND THEN I WAS SORRY

I could "say prayers" and "make a good Act of Contrition" as a child, but I didn't learn to pray until I was fourteen. My family had gone on a beach vacation where I met the beach bum of my dreams: older, tan, muscular, and bad. My mother took one look at him and declared him off-limits. That was all I needed to fuel my desire even further.

I waited until Mom and Dad went out and then snuck off to meet him. When my parents found out, they grounded me for the remainder of the week. That's when I learned to pray howling, sobbing prayers of woe. I prayed nonstop that Mom would let me out of my beachfront "prison." I was *heartily* sorry — sorry that I got caught.

My prayer life continued along that vein for the next nine years. Then at age twenty-three I started thinking about all my sin — everything I had done and thought and all the good I had failed to do. This time I didn't have to make anything up; I had plenty of real sins to confess.

And I was sorry. Truly, heartily sorry. For the first time, I was sorry I had offended God. The weight of my sin broke my heart and drove me to my knees.

"Jesus, save me!" I cried, even though at the time I didn't know what that meant. I only knew that I wanted Jesus to save me more than I had ever wanted anything before or since.

ENTER ANOTHER SINFUL WOMAN

She recalled the first time she had allowed a man to touch her. He had been drinking, a friend of her father. As he reclined at her family's table, she tried to rush past him on her way into the kitchen. When her father wasn't looking, the man reached out his hand and patted her thigh.

At first she was startled, but then she became curious. The rest of the evening she found reasons to brush past him. Every time she would catch his eye, she would smile and then look away, as if turning her head would turn away the thoughts that were making her uncomfortable but that she didn't want to give up altogether.

Finally, as her mother and father retired for the evening and bid good night to their guest, the young woman offered to check on the livestock in the pen.

"That's a good girl," her father said through his yawning.

Later, she heard those words again, only this time they came from the lips of her father's drunken friend as he touched her in a way that she instinctively knew was wrong.

"Ah, that's a good girl," he said and gave her a silver coin. "This will be our secret — and there's plenty more where this came from."

Her heart beat faster. *This isn't so bad after all,* she thought.

Now, many years and many men with silver coins later, she only thought about ending it. She felt dirty and defiled. The same men who visited her by night walked right past her during the daytime, not even acknowledging that she existed. Some would even pull their wives and children close and warn them against getting too close to the "sinful woman." Their wives would make clucking sounds, like a bunch of gossipy old hens.

What had begun as an easy way to make money and gain men's attention had turned into a trap. A pit. It was as if she was in a pit so deep that she couldn't even see sunlight. Every day she would try to claw her way out, only to be drawn back deeper by the sin tied like a weight around her ankles.

Then Jesus came.

She had overheard people in the marketplace talking about this "man of God who forgives sins." Some talked about him with scorn and derision, but others spoke in awe and reverence.

Day after day, as the weight of her sin crushed her, she would strain to hear more about this Jesus who forgave people's sins.

"Jesus, save me!" she found herself whispering as she lay awake one night. Even though she didn't fully understand what her prayer meant, she knew without a doubt that her sin was against God and God alone. With her heart broken and contrite, no one had to tell her to "make a good Act of Contrition." Words of repentance and contrition spilled from her lips as she confessed everything she had ever done or failed to do.

When she had finished, it was as if God himself had taken the whole lot and hurled it into the sea, and along with it, the weight that had dragged her down all those years. For the first time since she had been a child in her father's house, she slept in peace, wrapped in the love of her Savior.

CRASHING A DINNER PARTY

Upon awakening, the woman looked around, as if to see whether the weight of her sin was still with her. She remembered how she had prayed, "Jesus, save me!" and hoped it hadn't been a fluke, a brief moment of forgiveness and freedom from sin. She held her breath, waiting for the all too familiar feelings of guilt and shame to set in. When they didn't, she allowed herself to revel in this strange newness. She felt . . . saved. Forgiven. Redeemed. Restored. Brand new.

She held her breath, waiting for the all too familiar feelings of guilt and shame to set in. When they didn't, she allowed herself to revel in this strange newness.

A "good" girl.

She remembered, too, the one time she had seen Jesus. He had glanced her way for only a second, but in that short time, she felt as if he had read her thoughts and knew everything that was in her heart — and how it didn't seem to repulse him. Instead, she thought he had looked at her with love. However, she quickly brushed such thoughts away. *A man of God would never love a woman like me.*

Later that day, she learned that Jesus had been invited to a man named Simon's for dinner. She knew Simon well. *Some big shot at the synagogue. For all his religion . . . let's just say he thinks everyone else's breath stinks but his own,* she thought. *But Simon or no Simon, I need to see Jesus. I need to know if I'm really forgiven or just imagining this wonderful feeling.*

Then, grabbing an alabaster jar of expensive perfume, she ran all the way to Simon's house. Past the stares and whispers of the other dinner guests, the woman stopped short and fell at the feet of the One she had come to see and wept.

Although the Bible doesn't say if she even spoke to Jesus, her actions reveal a heart overcome with gratitude and brokenness. Perhaps she cried out the words of the psalmist, "For the sake of your name, O LORD, forgive my iniquity, though it is great" (Psalm 25:11).

As her tears dropped on Jesus' feet, she wiped them with her hair, kissed them, and poured perfume on them. Without him saying a word, she knew he was the One who had forgiven her. The One who had made her feel newer and cleaner than she had ever felt before. It was as if she and Jesus were the only ones in the room. She didn't care what anyone thought. She was forgiven!

Jesus, however, cared what Simon was thinking. In Simon's typical, self-satisfied way, he sniffed. *Ha!* he thought. *It doesn't take a prophet to see what kind of trash this woman is who's stinking up my house with this tearful display.*

Jesus turned to him and said, "Simon, I have something to tell you." Then he told his dinner host about two men with great debts. One owed ten thousand dollars and the other owed only one thousand dollars. Neither of them, however, had the money to pay his debt and faced a lifetime in prison. Then the moneylender surprised them both by canceling their debts.

"Which of them will love him more?" Jesus asked Simon.

"I suppose the one who had the bigger debt canceled."

Bingo!

Next, Jesus turned to the woman and pointed out to Simon that he hadn't offered to wash his feet, but that the woman washed his feet with her own tears. "Therefore, I tell you, her many sins have been forgiven — for she loved much," Jesus said. "But he who has been forgiven little loves little."

Then Jesus said to the woman, "Your sins are forgiven. Your faith has saved you; go in peace" (Luke 7:36–50).

I'M "NOT SO BAD" . . . RIGHT?

Just when I think I've got this sin thing licked, God shows me just how far I have yet to go. Sometimes I think my sins are "NBDs" (No Big Deals). I don't rob banks; I don't shoot up heroin. I don't say any of the really bad words. I don't get drunk or gamble at the racetrack. I don't even buy lottery tickets. Compared to some, maybe compared to most, I'm not so bad. The only thing wrong with that line of thinking is that I *am* "so bad." I'm so bad that if God were to show me exactly how bad I am, it would kill me.

How thankful I am that he only shows me my sin a few glimpses at a time. He does that usually when I'm feeling self-satisfied and smug, much as Jesus did with Simon.

Just recently, I had been feeling particularly good about myself when my daughter caught me taking a packet of Sweet'N Low from a restaurant and putting it in my purse. I had run out at home and rather than stop at the store on the way home from our lunch date, I didn't even think twice about taking the sweetener. It didn't bother me a bit until Laura gasped. "Mom! I can't believe you're stealing Sweet'N Low!" she cried. Everyone in the restaurant turned to look.

"What? It's just one packet," I said. Embarrassed, I put the Sweet'N Low back, but not before she launched into a tirade about how, as a waitress, she gets fed up with people pocketing napkins and silverware and saltshakers. "And now my own mother steals Sweet'N Low!"

Somehow I knew my "It's just one packet" didn't matter. Stealing is stealing, and God used my daughter to show me that in my heart, I'm a Sweet'N Low thief. The prophet Jeremiah got it right when he said the heart is "deceitful above all things and beyond cure" (Jeremiah 17:9). Other Bible translations say the heart is "desperately sick" (NASB), "hopelessly dark and deceitful" (MESSAGE), and "exceedingly perverse, and corrupt severely, mortally sick" (AMPLIFIED).

> *Somehow I knew my "It's just one packet" didn't matter. Stealing is stealing, and God used my daughter to show me that in my heart, I'm a Sweet'N Low thief.*

My heart is so deceitful that I can fool myself into thinking it's not, that I'm "not so bad" when I'm really "bad to the bone."

REAL JOY IS . . .

Several years ago I spoke at a women's retreat where their theme was "Experiencing the Joy!" I remember telling them that "real joy is knowing the depth of your sin and the extent of your idolatry." Until you believe with your whole being that, given the right set of circumstances, you are capable of committing any sin, and until you know that apart from Christ there is nothing that's naturally good in you, then you will never know real joy.

Real joy is knowing how bad I am and then comparing it to how much I have been forgiven. Jesus said it himself: Those who have been forgiven much, love much. Their gratitude spills over, and they find themselves crazy in love with God, falling at his feet, worshiping with abandon. They find themselves loving others extravagantly and forgiving others from the heart. For not only do those who have been forgiven much love much, but they forgive much too. As the Bible instructs, we are to "be kind and compassionate to one another, forgiving each other, just as in Christ God forgave you" (Ephesians 4:32).

HOW MUCH HAVE I BEEN FORGIVEN?

Compared to the woman at Jesus' feet, Simon's love was minuscule. Jesus had said he had only been forgiven little. Does that mean that the woman was a bigger sinner? Or was Jesus trying to tell Simon something else?

Although some sins are more heinous than others — murder is more detrimental to society than entertaining lustful thoughts or stealing a packet of Sweet'N Low — all sin is grievous to God. All sin separates us from him. All sin is serious.

Let's say that I had managed to keep the law perfectly, in my thoughts as well as in my deeds, the only exception being that one Sweet'N Low incident. If that were the only sin I ever committed, it would be that tiny pink packet in my purse that nailed Jesus to the cross. He died for my Sweet'N Low theft. He died for the time I snuck out of the beach house and disobeyed my parents. He died for all the times I pretended not to hear someone asking for help and all the times I tried to hide an unnecessary mall purchase from my husband.

In that way, my "little" sins are perhaps even more damnable than those of the prostitute on the street or the killer behind bars. Jesus, crucified for my laziness. Jesus, crucified for my gossip. Jesus, crucified for my tossing gum wrappers out the car window or boasting about my life.

It's not so much that Simon's sin was less than that of the "sinful" woman. Rather, it's that Simon couldn't or wouldn't see his sin as clearly as the woman saw hers. Real joy is knowing the depth of your sin and the extent of your idolatry, and then realizing the greatness of God's forgiveness.

Whenever my heart starts to grow cold, when I take comfort in being "not so bad" and seek satisfaction in feeling superior to others, all I need is to look at the cross of Christ. Then, once I see clearly that it was me who put Jesus there, I remember his words to another sinful woman: "Your sins are forgiven.... Your faith has saved you; go in peace" (Luke 7:48, 50).

A prayer of genuine contrition is one that God always welcomes. Like the woman at the feet of Jesus discovered, it's a prayer that brings relief and release, peace, pardon, and reconciliation. It's a prayer that acknowledges God's rightful place as Judge and ourselves as the ones most deserving of his judgment.

It's a prayer that trusts and embraces the words of the psalmist: "The sacrifices of God are a broken spirit; a broken and contrite heart, O God, you will not despise" (Psalm 51:17). It's a prayer that brings real joy.

So, break me, Lord! That I may know such joy.

Lord,

As I consider the story of this sinful woman at the feet of Jesus, I'm touched by her expression of love and gratitude. Such joy that springs from genuine sorrow over sin! How easy it is to grow callous over my own sin and to think of myself as "not so bad." Yet how clearly I see the sin of those around me.

Open my eyes, Lord, to see my sin and to hate it as much as you do. Teach me what it means to repent. For it's only when I see my sin as great that I can appreciate your even greater forgiveness, for it is vast. As far as the east is from the west, you say that's how far you remove my sin when I come to you for forgiveness.

A broken spirit and a contrite heart are precious to you. Dear Lord, I offer you mine.

In Jesus' name I pray. Amen.

DIGGING DEEPER

Think: Be truthful: When you consider your sin, how much do you grieve over it?

Study: Psalm 51

Apply: Use Psalm 51 as your prayer and pray your repentance to God.

Consider: It's God's kindness, not his anger, that breaks us and leads us to repentance.

Reflect: "Recognition of sin forces an awareness of God and develops an unhesitating trust in God's mercy."–Eugene Peterson

THE PRAYER OF ANNA

She Prayed with Persistence

*I wait for the LORD, my soul waits, and in his word
I put my hope. My soul waits for the Lord more
than watchmen wait for the morning.*

Psalm 130:5–6

At eighty-four, her fingers bent and her back bowed with age, the prophetess Anna, from the tribe of Asher, made her way to her usual place of worship inside the temple. Widowed after only seven years of marriage, she had spent most of her life here, worshiping day and night, fasting, and praying ceaselessly.

She prayed for a baby.

Not one for herself, but for *the* baby, the long-awaited "redemption of Israel" and the One who would be the Redeemer. In all the years she had spent in the temple in Jerusalem, she had seen many young couples bring their firstborn infant sons to consecrate them to the Lord. She had even seen many of these same baby boys return as grown men with wives and infant sons of their own. With each tiny cry from within a blanketed bundle in a proud father's arms, Anna's heart would beat a bit faster as she drew near to catch a glimpse.

Lord, is this the One? she would say to herself.

And with each one, the Lord would let her know, *No, not this one. Not yet. But keep praying, Daughter. Keep watching. Keep waiting. I won't be late; I promise.*

With that, she would go back to her accustomed place and continue her praying.

PLEASE, CHRISTMAS, DON'T BE LATE!

Is there anything more agonizing for a child than waiting for Christmas to arrive? I remember as a child when my sister and two brothers and I would alternate between agony and ecstasy every December as we anticipated the arrival of Christmas. With each day's waiting more torturous than the next, we would put our David Seville and the Chipmunks album on the hi-fi and commiserate with them as they pleaded, "Please, Christmas, don't be late!"

We would stare longingly at the calendar or at the clock or at the gifts underneath the Christmas tree, hoping the sheer force of our desire would make the time speed by. Every morning, even before our feet hit the floor, one of us would call out, "Dad, is it Christmas yet?"

Every morning, to our disappointment, our father would answer, "Not yet."

We wanted so badly for Christmas to come!

One year on Christmas Eve, the four of us got up at five in the morning. We sneaked into the living room and sat in front of the tree with ants in our pants. We sniffed the packages with our names on them, poked at the tape, and licked the ribbon.

It was coming, Christmas was coming, and we could feel it "groaning in our bones" (as our grandpa used to say).

We tried to control our anticipation and keep quiet, but four squirmy siblings itching to rip into Christmas loot are anything but quiet. Mom got up and shooed us back to bed — and then banned us from the living room for the rest of the day.

It was the single, longest day of the O'Brand children's lives.

As a four- or seven- or ten-year-old, it's hard to wait for Christmas. We don't like waiting! It's tempting to think Christmas isn't coming at all this year. Maybe not ever.

Two thousand years ago, the people of Israel longed for Christmas to come, too, although they didn't have a date on a calendar in order to count the days. They didn't even know it was Christmas they were waiting for. They only knew they had a groaning in their bones and a longing for the Promised One who would bring them redemption. They longed for a Redeemer and Rescuer. It was during this time of waiting that Anna served the Lord in the temple.

At Christmas, we sing, "O come, O come, Emmanuel!" The writer describes Israel as mourning in "lonely exile" and depicts the Jews as pleading for God to "ransom" them and to "free Thine own from Satan's tyranny."

Israel, once mighty and powerful over its enemies, had been enslaved, oppressed, and harassed by a succession of kings and despots and nations. At the time of Anna, Rome was Israel's oppressor. As a nation, Israel was without a king from their own people and, in the minds of many, without hope.

It had been so long since God had answered their prayers as a people that perhaps many had given up praying. *What's the use? God is either deaf or uninterested. He's not going to save us, so why bother even asking anymore?*

Some may have thought that, but not Anna. On the contrary, perhaps the longing and the waiting only fueled her anticipation and determination and made her prayers more fervent and persistent. Although we're not told exactly what she prayed, perhaps she used words from the psalms as her prayers, which was common practice in temple worship.

Perhaps as each new baby boy was brought to the temple, upon seeing that it was not *the* long-expected baby, Anna would raise her hands toward heaven and cry, "I wait for the LORD, my soul waits, and in his word I put my hope. My soul waits for the Lord more than watchmen wait for the morning" (Psalm 130:5–6).

Although Anna didn't know when the baby would come, she was confident that he would, just as surely as we know today that Christmas comes on December 25. Even though it had been hundreds of years since God had promised a Redeemer, the Child born of a virgin, the "sign of Immanuel," as foretold by the prophet Isaiah, Anna did not doubt that God would keep his promise. He always had, and she knew he always would.

It was Anna's role to not give up hoping that she would live to see God's promised Messiah, to keep praying for his coming, and to keep on worshiping, no matter what her circumstances.

WHEN THE ANSWER IS LONG IN COMING

One of the most frustrating aspects of the Christian life is waiting for God to answer your prayers and having them seem to go unanswered. When that happens, it's as if it's December 22 and you're seven years old all over again, waiting for

Christmas to arrive so you can tear into your presents and play with your toys. The difference is, when you're waiting for Christmas, you know when it will arrive. But when you're waiting on a prayer to be answered, you can't be sure that you'll ever see the answer you want or expect. That's because God is God and you are not, and he does as he sees fit. So you can pray from now until the day you die to win the Publisher's Sweepstakes, but if it's not in God's sovereign plan, you are not going to get that check for seventy-eight million dollars.

Although some things we pray for are in God's plan, because we're not made privy to his calendar, it may only appear that the Lord is not answering. When the answer is long in coming, when God doesn't answer as we hope or expect, it's easy to become disappointed or disillusioned. *Lord, I've been praying and praying about this thing for years, and you still haven't answered! Are you even listening?*

The more silent God seems, the more tempting it is to allow disappointment to turn to discouragement. *I knew you wouldn't answer my prayer. I'm trying to do everything right; I'm trying to have faith, but....*

Discouragement, if unchecked, easily turns to despair. *I can't go on. Why bother praying anymore? Nothing's going to ever change.*

But God tells us to ask, seek, and knock (Luke 11:9), to come to his throne (Hebrews 4:16; 10:19–22), and to pray continually (1 Thessalonians 5:17). We are to do all this even when we don't see any signs that God is at work or that he hears us.

For most of our married life, my husband and I have lived spiritually "mismatched." Neither of us were Christians when we married in 1975, but three years into the marriage, God called me into a relationship with him through faith in

Christ. Ever since then, my longtime fervent prayer for my husband has been for him to come to understand the depth of God's love for him and to receive that love through his own faith in Christ. More than anything, I want him to experience the smile of God on his life and to be sure of a place in heaven when he dies.

As I watch the years, then the decades, pass, sometimes I get a "groaning in my bones." I think about all that he's missing out on, and I long for him to want it for himself. He loves that I have an active faith, but he just doesn't seem to want one of his own. At least, that's how it appears to me.

However, how things look on the outside sometimes doesn't reflect what's going on inside or behind the scenes. That's where persistence comes in. Just as Anna must have discovered throughout her years of praying, not one year — not one day — was wasted. As for me, my time spent praying for this one thing has been time spent growing in my faith and in my knowledge of who God is and who he wants to be in my life. I have gone from hand-wringing laments over my situation to realizing what a gift my marriage is. I have discovered that it is possible to be genuinely content in waiting.

Even so, praying persistently can get discouraging at times, especially when you see how God answers others' prayers. Sometimes people pray for their loved ones and see them come to faith almost as soon as the prayer leaves their lips. Some pray for healing and people get healed. Other times, months, years, decades of praying go by without any indication that God even hears.

That's why in his Sermon on the Mount Jesus encouraged his listeners to ask, seek, and knock — not just once, but regularly, fervently. Not because by doing so we twist God's arm or wear him down with our asking, but to remind ourselves that he is almighty. If our prayers are "late" in being answered, they're only late to our finite understanding. God's answers are never late. He never says, "Oops"; he's always right on time.

Long-awaited answers stretch our faith and increase our endurance. Our perseverance produces character and character produces hope. "And hope does not disappoint us, because God has poured out his love into our hearts by the Holy Spirit, whom he has given us" (Romans 5:5). And that's really all we want — to know that we are loved and that God will take care of us.

> *God's answers are never late. He never says, "Oops"; he's always right on time.*

As for answers to our prayers, the richest answers are often not the speediest. "A prayer may be all the longer on its voyage because it is bringing us a heavier freight of blessing," noted theologian Charles Spurgeon once said. "Delayed answers are not only trials of faith, but they give us an opportunity of honoring God by our steadfast confidence in Him under apparent repulses." Anna knew this and lived to see the answer to her prayer to see the Messiah.

FIXING OUR EYES ON JESUS

Often when an answer to prayer is long in coming, there's a temptation to focus on the prayer itself or on the reason for praying — what I want — and not on the Lord. *Maybe I'm not using the right words,* I may think. *Maybe I don't have enough faith. Maybe if I put some extra money in the offering next Sunday or am nicer to my kids, I will see my answer.*

I may search the Internet for the newest, surefire way to get quick answers to prayer. I may even beg and plead with God to please, please, pleeeeeze answer my prayer just this one time and promise I'll never ask him for another thing. But often the answer I want doesn't come, and all God says is, "Be still before the LORD and wait patiently for him" (Psalm 37:7).

If there's one key to delayed answers to prayer, it's this: We must not fix our eyes on our prayer or its answer; we must fix our eyes on the Lord. We wait for *him*. Waiting, then, is not burdensome because I wait for God himself, the One who meets all my needs and is never late or incomplete in his coming.

It's my opinion that the measure of one's ability to wait patiently in a situation is proportionate to the measure of one's belief in the absolute sovereignty of God. Because he is sovereign, because he is in charge of the universe and not one molecule escapes his notice, because his love and goodness compel him to do what's best for his children, because he will never forget or forsake those he calls his own, I can leave the outcomes to him. That way, whatever the answer is, however long it takes, my faith stays stable because my faith is not in my prayer but in Christ. And when my focus and faith are in Christ, I am never disappointed, no matter how long I wait and pray — or even if the answer I want never comes. I will always have Christ.

> *And when my focus and faith are in Christ, I'm never disappointed, no matter how long I wait and pray — or even if the answer I want never comes.*

WHILE U WAIT

Anna spent nearly her entire life in the temple, worshiping night and day, fasting and praying. God had called her to a set-apart life. He was her Husband, who provided for her needs. Each day she awoke to his heartbeat and sought ways to draw close, to honor him with her life. Daily she persevered in prayer for the deliverance and redemption of her people and waited for God's answer.

While she waited, however, she didn't stagnate. Perhaps as she took notice of the people who made their pilgrimages to the temple and heard their stories of Roman oppression and outrageous taxation, and as she witnessed the strife among families and sensed the futility of their lives, she would bow her head and pray: "Hear us, O Shepherd of Israel. . . . Awaken your might; come and save us" (Psalm 80:1–2). Hers was a life of intercession.

Not many of us are called to a cloistered life. Unlike Anna, who was able to focus solely on the Lord, waiting on him and for him, most of us have jobs, families, and communities. We don't have the luxury of living, night and day, devoted to worship and prayer. Even so, the Bible instructs us: "Be joyful always; pray continually; give thanks in all circumstances" (1 Thessalonians 5:15–18), as we wait for him. As we do, we must not fret or worry or seek our own answers by our own means. God may call us to fast, but we are not to put our trust in our fasting. Sometimes God may call us to do nothing as we pray and wait; other times he may call us to action.

When the answer is long in coming, we need to keep our eyes fixed on the Lord, study his Word for his instruction, comfort, and encouragement, and pray about our prayers: *Lord, what would you have me do or say? Open the doors that you want me to go through; shut the ones you know I shouldn't. Give me words to speak — keep my mouth closed.* Then we need to trust that the Lord can and will do that which he deems best.

As Solomon wrote, "There is a time for everything, and a season for every activity under heaven" (Ecclesiastes 3:1), and "He has made everything beautiful in its time" (Ecclesiastes 3:11). It's often in the waiting that we receive some of God's most beautiful blessings. We discover that we can endure — with hope and perseverance, patience and joy. We discover that in the waiting, God himself is enough to sustain us, that his grace, indeed, is sufficient, and that he is all we ever need.

WHEN THE ANSWER COMES

"Long lay the world in sin and error pining," goes the Christmas carol "O Holy Night." With the birth of the long-awaited Savior comes a "thrill of hope, the weary world rejoices." Then the command: "Fall on your knees!"

Likewise, for more than sixty years Anna prayed for her world, which was "in sin and error pining." Perhaps she prayed, "Restore us, O God Almighty; make your face shine upon us, that we may be saved" (Psalm 80:7). *Send your Messiah, dear Lord! Be our Immanuel. Send your light into our darkness.*

Then one day, he appeared. God had come! He had answered Anna's prayer for the redemption of Israel with himself. Because she had spent those long decades in his presence, she recognized him immediately, a baby wriggling in a blanket.

Anna approached Mary and Joseph and beheld the answer to her long-awaited prayer. Perhaps she laughed with delight. Perhaps she cried with joy. We know "she gave thanks to God." After that she "spoke about the child to all who were looking forward to the redemption of Jerusalem" (Luke 2:38). She couldn't remain silent — she had seen the

Lord! Into the darkness, God had become the light, and he let an old woman see.

Often the answer to our prayers comes when all appears bleakest, when hope is laughable. Then when God answers, it can't be explained away. "The Lord did it!" is the only acceptable response, and we fall on our knees. Our faith buoyed, praise springs forth.

What about you? Are you praying for a person or a situation and are growing weary because the answer is long in coming? Take heart. The Lord has not forgotten you. Anna prayed for more than sixty years before she saw the answer to her prayer.

> *Often the answer to our prayers comes when all appears bleakest, when hope is laughable.*

"But when the time was right, God sent his Son" (Galatians 4:4 CEV), wrote the apostle Paul. When the time is right, he will answer you, too. That's when you will discover his answer to your prayer has been with you all along: Christ, always, only, and forever.

Lord,

I don't like the word "persistence" because it sounds too much like "patience," and patience means waiting — and I'm tired of waiting! It's difficult to keep praying when I don't see answers. It's discouraging and disheartening to see the prayers of others answered while I keep praying and praying and....

But that's because I'm looking through finite eyes while you, Lord, have the eyes of eternity, and you know best. Besides, I know that it's often in the waiting that I receive some of your greatest blessings. How else would I know that I can endure with hope and persevere with patience and joy unless I had been made to wait?

So, I confess my frustration and impatience and ask that you be my peace and my sufficiency. "Restore [me], O God Almighty; make your face shine upon [me]." It's you I wait for. It's you I seek.

In Jesus' name. Amen.

DIGGING DEEPER

Think: What are some of your "unanswered" prayers?

Study: Psalm 130

Apply: Read Anna's story in Luke 2:22–38. What inspiration can you gain from her prayer life for your own as you face long-awaited answers?

Consider: God in his wisdom often withholds or delays an answer to our requests because it would otherwise be harmful to us.

Reflect: "The value of persistent prayer is not that he will hear us ... but that we will finally hear him."–William McGill

THE PRAYER OF MARTHA

She Prayed with Hope

*I believe that you are Christ, the Son of God. You are
the one we hoped would come into the world.*
                                    John 11:27 (CEV)

At the risk of sounding irreverent or insensitive, I love
funerals at my church. My pastor usually begins by saying, as we celebrate our brother or sister's life, it's okay to
laugh, and it's okay to cry. Then as he talks about the one
who has left us, he almost always includes funny stories.

We laugh . . . and we cry. We say, "Too bad _____
isn't here to see this. He/she would enjoy it."

My friend Velda Dyer says she wants balloons and con-
fetti at her funeral. She says she's thinking about selling tickets, and she wants only handsome men to carry her coffin.
We make light of our funeral talk, but at the same time, we
know all too well the pain that accompanies death. We've
held new widows as they've cried, and we've stood by parents as they've buried their children.

Death, although a part of life, is an enemy. It's unnatural. We were made to live forever, and we grieve because we don't — not here on earth anyway.

Often during a funeral my pastor will tell us that we should all meet in heaven at the east gate. We'll have a Seven Rivers Presbyterian Church contingent. Those who go on before the rest of us can scope the place out and then wait, welcoming the rest of us with banners and signs. Then when we're all there safely, we'll have a party together.

No more pain, no more suffering. No more loneliness or grief. No more death, which tears at a heart with cruel abandon. We'll all be safely home.

Home with Christ.

That's our hope. *He* is our hope.

Just ask Martha.

MEETING MARTHA

Martha of Bethany knew all about hope. She frequently welcomed Jesus into her home, cooking for him and his friends and listening to their conversations about the kingdom of God being near.

As Jesus spoke, she noticed how different he was from the other religious leaders at the synagogue. They spouted their opinions as if they were gospel truth, but then changed them whenever a new idea came into vogue.

In sharp contrast, Jesus spoke with unwavering authority. He spoke truth, as if he were truth itself. His words actually brought life to the Holy Scriptures and life to everyone who listened and believed.

Jesus brought life to Martha — life and hope and a peace she had never known before. Martha knew beyond a doubt that this man who considered her a dear friend was the One, the Christ of God, whom the Jews had been hoping would come. With Jesus in their midst, with him in her home and in her life, Martha knew no harm could ever come near her.

Often as she scurried around her kitchen, preparing a meal for Jesus and his band of men, Martha recalled the words of Psalm 33:20–22:

> We wait in hope for the LORD;
>> he is our help and shield.
> In him our hearts rejoice,
>> for we trust in his holy name.
> May your unfailing love rest upon us, O LORD,
>> even as we put our hope in you.

The hope of Israel — in my living room, she would think and shake her head in wonder. *Imagine that!*

WISHING AND HOPING AND IMPOSSIBLE IMPOSSIBILITIES

Recently, I joined a new gym. Four or five times a week I go and work out, hoping to lose weight and lower my cholesterol. I'm hoping that by summer I won't look too terrible in my bathing suit.

I'm also hoping that our younger daughter will move out on her own this year. I'm hoping to turn her room into a den — and I'm hoping that my husband isn't serious about painting a Tampa Bay Buccaneers emblem on our back porch floor!

I'm hoping to see my daughter Alison and my granddaughter, Caroline, soon, hoping that my son-in-law, Craig, gets the promotion he's hoping for, and hoping that the price will go down on the digital camera I found for sale on the Internet.

I say I'm hoping for all these things to happen, but what I really mean is that I'm wishing that they will happen. Wishing has that wistful "if only" quality to it. It's a passive, "Maybe someday it will come true" thought. A wish is a yearning or desire that may or may not come true. Hope, on the other hand, goes beyond mere wishing. Biblical hope is a certainty, usually in the face of impossibility.

The ancient prophet Daniel faced certain death. As an Israelite living in Babylon, Daniel was thrown into a lions' den for refusing to stop worshiping God. His hope was that God could spare him if he wanted to, or else that he would die and be with God forever in glory. Either way, whatever the outcome, he put his hope in God. The next morning, Daniel was found alive, without even a scratch on him. God had spared his life.

The Bible records others who faced impossibilities. In writing about Abraham, the great patriarch of the faith, the apostle Paul writes, "Against all hope, Abraham in hope believed" (Romans 4:18). God had told this childless, impotent old man that he would father a nation, with his childless, old wife, who was well past her childbearing years. Talk about impossibilities!

That's what makes hope more than mere wishing. As English author G. K. Chesterton once said, "Hope means hoping when things are hopeless, or it is no virtue at all. . . . As long as matters are really hopeful, hope is mere flattery or platitude; it is only when everything is hopeless that hope begins to be a strength."

Real hope flies in the face of reason or even common sense and contrary to probability or even possibility. When everyone around you says it can't be done, hope says, "Maybe so, but you don't know what God can do."

"When God is about to do something great, he starts with a difficulty," said the late Lutheran pastor Armin Gesswein. "When he is about to do something truly magnificent, he starts with an impossibility." As Martha was about to see, hope can even bring death back to life.

> *When everyone around you says it can't be done, hope says, "Maybe so, but you don't know what God can do."*

WHEN HOPE IS GONE, HOPE KEEPS HOPING

Martha's brother, Lazarus, had fallen ill. Martha and her sister, Mary, both cared for him day and night, praying and hoping, wishing for him to get well. Never one to give up, Martha did all she could do to nurse him back to health, but nothing she did seemed to help. Thus, as life ebbed from her beloved brother, Martha sent someone to go find Jesus. She knew he would drop whatever he was doing and rush to his friend's aid and heal Lazarus.

That was Martha's hope.

However, when Jesus received Martha's message, "Lord, the one you love is sick," he didn't drop everything to rush to Bethany. All he said was, "This sickness will not end in death. No, it is for God's glory so that God's Son may be glorified through it" (John 11:3–4). Then, despite his love for Martha and her brother and sister, or perhaps because of it, he stayed where he was for two more days.

Meanwhile, Martha waited and hoped. She knew all about other times when Jesus had healed people, even strangers. *Surely he will spare dear Lazarus,* she thought as she put another cool cloth across her brother's forehead. *After all, we're friends.*

As Lazarus grew weaker, Martha kept one eye on him and one eye on the front door, hoping Jesus would enter at any moment. But Jesus didn't arrive in time, and Lazarus died.

Martha and her sister wrapped their dear brother's body in grave cloths, placed him in a tomb, had it sealed, then set about the painful process of grieving the one they loved. Martha had hoped that Jesus would heal her brother. She knew that he was more than able to, but she didn't know how he could have let her down as he did. Now she had to place her hope in eternity, that she would see her brother again . . . someday.

But today, she grieved, not just for her brother, but for her disappointment that Jesus had not come to her aid.

GIVING BIRTH TO HOPE

Her name was Hope. Two days after she was born, her parents, David and Nancy Guthrie, learned that their daughter had a rare metabolic disorder called Zellweger Syndrome, a disorder that is always fatal.

Many of their friends and even strangers began praying for Hope, praying in hope and with hope that God would miraculously heal this precious baby girl. However, the Guthries sensed that that might not be God's plan for them. Instead, their prayers for Hope were for strength for the journey that lay ahead and trust in the midst of their sorrow, difficulty, and disappointment.

They knew that if God did heal Hope, it would only be temporal. Like everyone, she would eventually die someday. But if he chose to let her die as an infant, that would mean ultimate, eternal healing, which would be far greater for their daughter. Either way, they prayed in hope.

Hope Guthrie lived on earth for 199 days. She now lives forever in heaven with her brother, Gabriel, who also died of Zellweger Syndrome, waiting to be reunited with her parents.

When it comes to hope and grief, the two are not mutually exclusive, like oil and water. For those who place their hope in God through faith in Christ, grief and hope can coexist. For those who die in Christ, we who are left behind to mourn their passing can, at the same time, cheer their "homegoing." That's what makes the funerals at my church so great. That's why Velda Dyer wants balloons. The hope that we have is for eternity. Forever and ever and ever and....

Even so, grief cuts like a rusty saw blade. It stings and throbs and bleeds. It sucks the life out of us and keeps sucking until we cry out for death itself to ease our pain. But for those who are in Christ, God himself brings hope, even in our sorrow and darkness.

When the ancient Job had everything but his life and a nagging wife taken from him all at once, through his incredible physical and emotional pain he cried out, "Though [God] slay me, yet will I hope in him" (Job 13:15). Our hope in suffering is not being confident that it will be taken away but that God will infuse it with his divine purpose, that he will use it for his glory and our good, and that his grace will be sufficient to see us through.

DEAD MAN WALKING . . . FILM AT ELEVEN

By the time Jesus arrived in Bethany, Lazarus had been dead for four days. He had known that and had even told his disciples days before that Lazarus had died. When Martha heard that Jesus was on his way to her house, she ran to meet him. In her grief she cried, "Lord, if you had been here, my brother would not have died." *Where were you? You were my one — my only — hope! Now it's too late.* "Yet even now I know that God will do anything you ask," she continued.

Jesus said to her, "Your brother will live again!"

"I know that he will be raised to life on the last day, when all the dead are raised," she replied.

"I am [the resurrection and the life,] the one who raises the dead to life!" Jesus said. "Everyone who has faith in me will live, even if they die. And everyone who lives because of faith in me will never really die. Do you believe this?"

Then Martha, in her grief and confusion, cried out a prayer, a declaration of hope: "Yes, Lord! . . . I believe that you are Christ, the Son of God. You are the one we hoped would come into the world" (John 11:17–27 CEV). Martha's prayer of hope focused on the God of hope, not in what she hoped would happen next.

Hope believes in spite of circumstances or feelings. Hope, in the face of hopelessness, holds the soul like an anchor, firm and secure (Hebrews 6:19). Hope looks through tears of grief and sorrow and sees Jesus — and rejoices. Our grief may be great, but because Jesus is our hope, our sorrow will not go on forever. Someday, all of our tears will be wiped away.

> *Hope looks through tears of grief and sorrow and sees Jesus — and rejoices.*

For Martha, her tears of grief were about to turn to tears of joy. As Jesus walked with Martha and Mary and the other mourners to the tomb where they buried Lazarus, Jesus became deeply moved in spirit and wept.

That, too, is our hope: that Jesus suffers the same human emotion as we suffer. He feels grief and sorrow and pain. He knows what it is to stand at the grave of a friend.

Jesus then ordered the stone seal to be removed from the tomb. And even though his friend had been dead for four days, he told Martha, "Did I not tell you that if you believed, you would see the glory of God?" (John 11:40). Then he called for Lazarus to come out of the tomb.

Everyone stood silent, afraid to breathe. Then . . . the dead man came to life. He walked out of his tomb, and because he did, Martha's hope was unbound and set free. Hope hadn't disappointed her after all. Hope himself had proven that he could conquer even death.

HOPE FOR TOMORROW, TODAY

The congregation of the Christian Reformed Church in Rochester, New York, was about to get a hands-on lesson about hope and dying and rising with Christ as their young preacher rose to speak on October 18, 1998. "I'm dying," the Rev. James Van Tholen told them. "Maybe it will take longer instead of shorter; maybe I'll preach for several months, maybe for a bit more. But I am dying. I know it, and I hate it, and I'm frightened by it. But there is hope, unwavering hope. I have hope, not in something I've done, some purity I've maintained, or some sermon I've written. I hope in God — the God who reaches out for an enemy, saves a sinner, dies for the weak. That's the gospel, and I can stake my life on it. I must. And so must you."

Van Tholen, whose last sermons are recorded in the book *Where All Hope Lies*, lost his battle with cancer in January 2001 at age thirty-six. Although he lost his life, he never lost his hope.

What is it that you need hope for? What impossibility do you face today? What in your life has you feeling hopeless, helpless, and in despair? As Martha did, instead of putting hope in a situation, we can put our situation in Hope's hands.

Our God is himself an anchor of hope, given to us to keep us moored to him. He grips us tightly, never letting go. He walks with us in our darkness and grief and holds us through our difficulties. He is stable and sure. He weeps with us; his presence comforts us.

We are never promised days without pain, only that God will give us strength to endure. That is our hope, and hope is what will see us not only through to the end but beyond to eternity.

Jesus, God of hope,

Even if you had never raised Lazarus back to life, Martha still would have hoped in you, because you were her hope. Likewise, you are my hope.

My hope is not that things will turn out the way I plan or want here on earth but that someday I will be Home. Safe with you, never to worry or grieve, hurt, fret, or despair again.

When life gets difficult, help me to remember that you are always good. Remind me that, because my hope is in you, that you will never disappoint me. You will never fail me.

I believe that you are Christ, the Son of God. You are the One I hoped would come into my world — and you did! Hallelujah, you did.

In Jesus' name I pray. Amen.

DIGGING DEEPER

Think: In what area of your life or in what situation do you lack hope? In what area are you most hopeful?

Study: Isaiah 40

Apply: What does it mean to hope in the Lord? As you think about it, express your thoughts to God as a prayer of hope.

Consider: Hope that is seen is no hope at all (Romans 8:24).

Reflect: "There is a difference between wishing and hoping: a wish is what we think will give us happiness; a hope is what we believe God will do to fulfill our lives. Wishes are based on human fantasies; hopes are based on God's promises."—Eugene Peterson

THE PRAYER OF MARY

She Prayed with Joy

*My soul glorifies the Lord and
my spirit rejoices in God my Savior.*

Luke 1:46–47

- "We regret to inform you. . . ."
- "The test results don't look good. . . ."
- "Mom, I'm pregnant. . . ."

It's easy to praise the Lord when all is well. When you're in love or when you're healthy and strong. When you enjoy your work, when the baby sleeps through the night and your eight-year-old finally puts his toys away and makes his bed without being told.

When you pray that the sun will shine for your planned picnic — and it does — you praise the Lord.

When you find a one-hundred-dollar error in your checkbook — in your favor — you praise the Lord.

When you finally lose those last ten stubborn pounds, and you can zip up your favorite jeans without inhaling until you pass out, you praise the Lord.

- I praise you, Lord, for the hollyhocks blooming in my yard.
- I praise you, Lord, for soft, furry kittens.
- I praise you, Lord, for ripe avocados and juicy navel oranges, for blue skies and Red Tag Sale Days at J. C. Penney.

We praise the Lord for all sorts of good things, as we should, but what about the gray days and the black nights? What about the spot on your liver and the termites in your basement? What about when you're out of food and out of money, out of breath and out of control? When the checks bounce and the sheriff leads your husband away in handcuffs, when your unmarried teenage daughter informs you that she's pregnant, what prompts your praise then?

When your world falls apart, is it even possible to praise the Lord?

FROM ORDINARY TO HIGHLY FAVORED

For Mary of Nazareth, life could be described in one word: ordinary. *But things are about to change,* she whispered to herself as she sorted through the box where she kept the linens and dishes and candlesticks she had been collecting practically since the day she was born, getting herself ready for her someday wedding day.

She hummed as she refolded her latest blanket for her marriage bed, then giggled at the thought of what that meant. She had heard some of the women talking, and she had seen their round, swollen bellies and had even helped at several births. And although she and her friends sometimes talked about what it all must be like, as a virgin she could only speculate.

Not for long, she thought. *Soon I'll be Mrs. Joseph the Carpenter. Then we'll have lots of fat babies, and they'll grow up and have their own fat babies, and I'll be Grandma Mary.* At that, she laughed out loud.

"Greetings, you who are highly favored!"

The voice startled her.

"The Lord is with you."

Mary gasped, frozen with fear. She sensed that the man who spoke posed no danger, but his greeting troubled her. *Highly favored? What does that mean?* she thought.

She waited for the stranger to reveal himself as part of a joke being played on her by one of her brothers, but she soon realized that this was no joke.

"Do not be afraid, Mary, you have found favor with God," he said.

Her mind raced. *Favor with God? I'm just a girl from Nazareth — a nobody.*

Then the stranger, an angel named Gabriel sent directly from God, announced the real reason for his visit: "You will be with child and give birth to a son, and you are to give him the name Jesus."

With child? Sure, after I'm married.

Gabriel continued. "He will be great and will be called the Son of the Most High. The Lord God will give him the throne of his father David, and he will reign over the house of Jacob forever; his kingdom will never end."

As Mary took in the angel's words one at a time, she tried to comprehend their strangeness. *"He will be great" — that's nice to know. "The Son of the Most High" — aren't we all sons and daughters of God? "His father David" — David? But I'm engaged to Joseph! Who's David?*

She gasped again. From all her years of listening to her father repeat the Scripture he had heard read at the temple, she recalled the stories of David, the king of Israel, and of the promised Messiah, who would be called "David's Son."

"Son of the Most High" — the Son ... of God?

As she tried to process this astounding announcement, she could only whisper, "How will this be ... since I am a virgin?"

The angel went on to explain how it would happen: She would remain a virgin, with the baby being conceived by a miracle of God, by the power of his Holy Spirit. That way, "the holy one to be born" would be the undisputed Son of almighty God (Luke 1:28–35).

The "sign of Immanuel, God with us." Mary recalled the words of the prophet Isaiah: "The virgin will be with child and will give birth to a son, and will call him Immanuel" (Isaiah 7:14). Mary and her friends used to laugh and say, "Maybe that will be me." But none of them seriously considered herself to be the chosen one to bear the Christ Child.

That would be ... impossible.

MISSION IMPOSSIBLE

In ancient Israel, the penalty for adultery was death by stoning. Even though Mary and Joseph were not yet married, only engaged, in their culture engagement was as binding a covenant as was marriage. At best, Mary becoming pregnant before marriage would cause certain ostracism from family and friends and divorce from Joseph. She would be the topic of gossip, labeled a common whore for the rest of her life. What the angel had proposed was by far the most *un*common occurrence anyone could ever have imagined.

"Even Elizabeth your relative is going to have a child in her old age," the angel reminded her.

Mary recalled Aunt Elizabeth telling the family about her pregnancy and how the news made Uncle Zechariah unable to speak. The family joke was, the miracle wasn't so much that Elizabeth was pregnant but that Zechariah was speechless. "That proves nothing is impossible with God!" her father had said.

As if reading her thoughts, the angel told her, "For nothing is impossible with God."

The virgin will be with child ... Immanuel ... Son of the Most High. As Mary pondered these strange, impossible, wonderful, terrifying thoughts, she found herself enveloped in a sense of peace unlike anything she had ever known. It was as if God himself had stepped into her room and permeated every corner with his glory. She could only describe it as a nearly unbearable joy. Her whole being cried out, "Yes!" in the presence of the Lord. Nothing would be too great a burden, nothing would be too difficult, nothing would be impossible — not even a virgin bearing the Son of God.

"I am the Lord's servant," she said. And the angel left her (Luke 1:36–38).

"Honey, We Have to Talk"

The Bible doesn't say anything about how Mary's family reacted to her news, but Joseph was deeply distressed. The law said Mary should be put to death, but he loved her too much for that, nor did he want to subject her to public disgrace. So, he decided to divorce her quietly, perhaps telling everyone, "It's not her; it's me. I'm just not ready for commitment, I guess."

As he grieved over the loss of his beloved wife-to-be and their future together, an angel of the Lord visited him and in a dream told him that the baby was, indeed, conceived by God's Spirit and that he, Joseph, would name the child Jesus. Savior. Son of the Most High. Son of God — God, the Son.

The impossible was about to become possible.

O MAGNIFY THE LORD

Meanwhile, Mary left town to visit with pregnant Aunt Elizabeth. When she arrived and called out a greeting, Elizabeth felt her own baby leap in her womb. That same "nearly unbearable joy" Mary had experienced filled her soul, too, and she cried, "Blessed are you among women, and blessed is the child you will bear! But why am I so favored, that the mother of my Lord should come to me?"

The past few months had been a roller coaster of emotion for Mary. Going from being an ordinary teenage girl planning her wedding to being the prophesied "virgin mother," she marveled at how God had taken care of every detail surrounding her pregnancy, down to assuring Joseph that she truly was telling the truth. Through the most difficult crisis of her life thus far, God had shown himself to be greater than she ever imagined.

Through the most difficult crisis of her life thus far, God had shown himself to be greater than she ever imagined.

As Elizabeth continued to bless Mary for believing God's words to her, Mary sang the prayer of praise that would be immortalized by becoming part of Holy Scripture: "My soul glorifies the Lord and my spirit rejoices in God my Savior, for he has been mindful of the humble state of his servant."

Mary praised the Lord for all he had done. She rejoiced because of who he was and is and always will be: mighty, holy, merciful. She recounted his justice and anger against the proud, how he lifts up the humble, how he "has filled the hungry with good things" and "has sent the rich away empty" (Luke 1:46–53).

Her song echoed the songs and psalms of God's people throughout the ages. As the psalmist David penned, "Let everything that has breath praise the LORD!" (Psalm 150:6). No matter what a person's circumstance, the call rings out, "Praise the Lord!"

"HOW CAN THIS BE?"

Amid the mice and filth of a Taliban prison in Afghanistan, two ordinary American young women wrote and sang praise songs to the Lord. Missionaries Dayna Curry, who battled loneliness, and Heather Mercer, who battled fear, didn't know their fate at the hands of their captors. Even so, in the midst of their uncertain future, the two found reason to pray rejoicing. They took comfort in recalling the biblical accounts of King David and of Job, both of whom wrestled with God because of their difficult circumstances, yet ultimately surrendered with praise to the Almighty.

"Even if we'd died in prison, even if the Taliban had killed us, God would still be good," said Heather. "God would still be who he says he is."

As for the ancient Job, after God had allowed all of his riches and even his children to be taken from him, covered with boils, plagued with a nagging wife and "who needs enemies"–type friends, he declared, "Though [God] slay me, yet will I hope in him" (Job 13:15). In his pain, he praised the Lord.

In his study of the psalms, *Prayers of the Heart*, author Eugene Peterson writes, "All prayer finally, in one way or another, becomes praise. No matter how much we suffer, no matter our doubts — everything finds its way into praise, the final consummating prayer."

He adds, "Not to say that other prayers are inferior to praise, only that prayer, pursued far enough, becomes praise." It's human nature for our prayers to begin with cries for mercy, comfort, and help. We pray in our pain and in our need. We pray in the midst of our sin. We plead for wisdom and strength, and we beg for peace in our confusion.

Perhaps as Mary experienced her first bout of morning sickness and the realization of what lay ahead for her hit like a wave of nausea, she cried out to God for his help. Chosen or not, she was human, just as we are. But just as her prayers and our prayers may begin with need, as Peterson says, pursued far enough, they become praise.

TURNING PRAYER TO PRAISE

Throughout the Bible, the term *praise* appears more than two hundred times, with the phrase "praise the LORD" appearing most often as a command. *People of God, give praise to the One who has redeemed you!* Although some commands to offer praise are prompted by awe and wonder at God's majesty, such as when the psalmist writes of shining stars and crashing waves, many are the result of a wrestling in prayer.

I especially love when King David starts a psalm with his feelings of confusion or fear, or even a plea for God to decimate his enemies on the spot, and then ends his psalm with praise. He starts:

O LORD, how many are my foes! (Psalm 3:1)

Give ear to my words, O Lord,
    consider my sighing. (Psalm 5:1)

Why, O Lord, do you stand far off?
    Why do you hide yourself in times of trouble? (Psalm
    10:1)

How long, O Lord? Will you forget me forever? (Psalm
    13:1)

Next, he pours out his anguish and his complaint. He lists his grievances and his sorrows. He does what we do when we come to the Father's throne. But his prayers don't stay laments. Sometimes right away, sometimes after many bitter words, David uses the word "but," and at that point his prayer becomes praise.

But you are a shield around me, O LORD. (Psalm 3:3)

But I, by your great mercy,
    will come into your house;
in reverence will I bow down.... (Psalm 5:7)

But you, O God, do see trouble and grief. (Psalm 10:14)

But I trust in your unfailing love;
    my heart rejoices in your salvation.
I will sing to the LORD,
    for he has been good to me. (Psalm 13:5–6)

In the hymn "How Sweet the Name of Jesus Sounds," John Newton writes:

Weak is the effort of my heart,
and cold my warmest thought;

but when I see Thee as Thou art,
I'll praise Thee as I ought.

The how-to of turning prayer to praise is in beholding God as he is.

Who is he? He is the Maker and Sustainer of every molecule of the universe. He is the kindest Father, the fairest Judge. He sees every struggle and feels every sorrow. He is All-powerful. He is Mercy. He is Love.

He is Seeker of the lost and Finder of the forgotten. He is Sharer of Wisdom, the Lover of those who desperately long to be loved. Our enemies become his enemies, and when he pursues them, he always wins.

> *He is the kindest Father, the fairest Judge. He sees every struggle and feels every sorrow. He is All-powerful. He is Mercy. He is Love.*

He is a Home Builder and a Fixer of broken people. He is Grace and Strength, Laughter and Hope.

When Mary turned her eyes toward God, when Dayna Curry and Heather Mercer focused their eyes on the Almighty, when Job said, "My ears had heard of you *but now my eyes have seen you*" (Job 42:5, emphasis mine), when King David and John Newton and you and I "see Thee as Thou art," when all of creation declares God's glory, that's when all prayer becomes praise. Whatever we face, whether good times or bad, nothing is impossible with God.

"Therefore, let everything that has breath praise the LORD. Praise the LORD" (Psalm 150:6).

O Most Holy God,

My soul, too, glorifies you, and my spirit rejoices in you, my Savior, for you have been and continue to be mindful of me. You alone are worthy. You alone are great. You alone speak creation into being and still the raging storms. You alone are able to topple a kingdom with a whisper.

You, Lord, stoop from heaven to lift up lowly people. You extend your mercy and lavish your grace. You do immeasurably more than we can ever think or imagine. Open my eyes to see you clearly, and touch my lips that, like Mary, my prayer will be one of praise to you. For you alone are worthy of praise.

In Jesus' name I praise you. Amen.

DIGGING DEEPER

Think: What inspires your heart to praise God?

Study: Psalm 103

Apply: In Mary's *Magnificat* found in Luke 1:46–55, Mary glorifies God by recounting his characteristics or attributes. In your own prayer of praise, tell God all the reasons you adore him.

Consider: One cannot praise God and complain at the same time.

Reflect: "No prayer of adoration will ever soar higher than a simple cry: 'I love you, God.'"—Louis Cassels

INDEX OF PRAYERS AND PRAISES
OF WOMEN IN THE BIBLE

The following index includes all the prayers and praises of women in the Bible. Note that while there are many godly women in biblical times, we are limiting this index to references to women actually praying. Although some of the comments in these passage are not actually prayers addressed to God, they do indicate a praising spirit that is brought before the throne of the Almighty. The names of those whose prayers are discussed in *Praying with Women of the Bible* are put in bold print, together with page references.

We want to hear from you. Please send your comments
about this book to us in care of zreview@zondervan.com.
Thank you.

GRAND RAPIDS, MICHIGAN 49530 USA

WWW.ZONDERVAN.COM